W9-AHI-648

"Peter Greer and David Weekley provide an invaluable guide for navigating the critical journey of successful board–CEO relationships. *The Board and the CEO* charts the course of making your organization much more effective in achieving your mission."

—Chris Crane, founder and CEO, Edify;
HOPE International board member

"Getting the board and CEO relationship right is essential for any high-impact business, university, or nonprofit. Yet too often, it veers off track causing unnecessary organizational mayhem. Based on years of experience both as a board member and as an organizational leader, Peter and David provide practical guidance on how to ensure this vital relationship stays on mission. Practical, concise, and relevant, boards and organizational leaders would be wise to invest time in reading this book."

–Kurt Keilhacker, board chair, Praxis

"Thanks so much to Peter and David for a fresh look at the relationship between nonprofit CEOs and their boards. *The Board and the CEO* will help any organization avoid mission drift and increase their impact."

–Durwood Snead, director of GlobalX,
North Point Community Church

"With this highly readable book, Peter Greer and David Weekley have given organizational leaders the gift of reflecting on their own extensive experience serving in CEO and board member capacities, respectively. They show why the board–CEO relationship is critical to an organization's success and provide blessedly practical action steps and assessments that could be applied in a variety of settings. As a board member I found the book clarifying and inspiring."

> –Katelyn Beaty, editor at large, Christianity Today magazine; HOPE International board member

"The single most important predictor of nonprofit vitality and long-term impact is healthy governance, yet governance is almost always underappreciated. *The Board and the CEO* is an indispensable resource for anyone willing to challenge the status quo with proven solutions so that our organizations can truly thrive."

> –Stephan Bauman, former president and CEO, World Relief; author, *Possible, Seeking Refuge,* and *Break Open the Sky*

The Board and the CEO

THE
BOARD
AND THE
CEO

Seven practices to protect your organization's
MOST IMPORTANT RELATIONSHIP

**PETER GREER &
DAVID WEEKLEY**

Foreword by Tiger Dawson

Copyright © 2017 Peter Greer and David Weekley
All rights reserved.

ISBN-10: 1547270160
ISBN-13: 978-1547270163

All rights reserved. No portion of this book may be
reproduced, stored in a retrieval system, or transmitted in any
form or by any means—electronic, mechanical, photocopy,
recording, scanning, or other—except for brief quotations in
critical reviews or articles, without the prior written
permission of the authors.

Publication, distribution, and fulfillment services provided
by CreateSpace, a DBA of On-Demand Publishing, LLC
(Scotts Valley, CA).
www.createspace.com

This book may be purchased in bulk for educational, business,
or promotional use. For information, please e-mail
peterkgreer@gmail.com

Cover design by Kelly Ryan.

Peter Greer's photo by Jeremy Cowart.

David Weekley's photo provided by David Weekly Homes.

Dedicated to Jeff Rutt for his visionary leadership
and trusted friendship.

Books by Peter Greer

The Giver and the Gift
(coauthored by David Weekley)

Created to Flourish
(coauthored by Phil Smith)

40/40 Vision
(coauthored by Greg Lafferty)

Mission Drift
(coauthored by Chris Horst with Anna Haggard)

The Spiritual Danger of Doing Good
(with Anna Haggard)

Entrepreneurship for Human Flourishing
(coauthored by Chris Horst)

Watching Seeds Grow
(coauthored by Keith Greer)

Mommy's Heart Went Pop!
(coauthored by Christina Kyllonen)

Books by David Weekley

The Giver and the Gift
(coauthored by Peter Greer)

How to Buy a Home Without Getting Hammered
(with Patrick Byers)

Contents

Foreword   9

Introduction   14

1. Mission, Not Ego   22

2. Clarity, Not Confusion   31

3. Consistent Communication, Not Mystery   43

4. Accountability, Not Platitudes   49

5. Healthy Conflict, Not Kumbaya   60

6. Prepared, Not Panicked   75

7. Involved, Not Detached   91

Conclusion   101

Acknowledgements   104

Appendix 1: Annual CEO/ED Evaluation   106

Appendix 2: Annual CEO/ED Self-Evaluation   110

Appendix 3: Annual Board Self-
Evaluation   115

Appendix 4: Board of Directors Survey   121

Appendix 5: Board Nomination Form   124

Appendix 6: Annual Board Member
Affirmation Statement   128

Appendix 7: Ten Board Member Profiles   130

Annotated Bibliography   132

Notes   137

About the Authors   140

About the Organizations   141

Related Works   142

FOREWORD

Early in my professional career, whenever I prepared agendas for business meetings, I would script the time with painstaking precision. From beginning to end, I liked to know the exact issues that would be covered, who would present them and in what order, the questions that would surface, and the decisions that would be reached by the end of the time.

Twenty-five years ago, I arrived prepared for my first meeting with David Weekley. I was working at the time for Young Life, a ministry focused on sharing God's love with adolescents, and David had agreed to review the strategic plan we were about to launch. True to form, I'd plotted the amount of time we'd use for introductions, for discussion of the plan, and for questions. If all went well, I also hoped to invite David to invest in our initiative, both as a financial partner and as a long-term advisor, drawing upon the significant insight and experience he'd gained from his business and nonprofit background. Nervous and excited, I arrived at David's office and after brief introductions, launched into describing this new plan that would double the impact of Young Life in Houston in eight years. David listened intently. Everything was going according to plan.

Suddenly, the course of the meeting shifted unexpectedly. David kindly and boldly began to pepper me with questions: What kind of board members will you need to accomplish this? What are your sources for funding? Can you achieve the same results in four years instead of eight?

Over the next hour, as my agenda went out the window, a dynamic conversation of questions, answers, and new ideas unfolded.

As our meeting drew to a close, David asked what he could do for me. Recalling my elaborate master plan, I said that we obviously needed funds to carry out the initiative, but, even more, we'd love for David to consider giving his time and strategic advice as well. David asked how much time I was thinking. I suggested meeting once a quarter would be adequate. "That's not nearly enough time!" he replied emphatically. "If you want to do this right and have a true impact, we need to meet at least a few hours a month." Though his response surprised me, I was thrilled.

This began a series of monthly meetings around growing an effective organization—and along the way, we built a great friendship. As I prepared each month to go to David's office, I would still meticulously plan the beginning, the middle, and the end of our time together, but somehow, our meetings never quite worked out as I expected. Somewhere just past the beginning, they always went in a totally different and wonderful direction. David would ask great questions—ones I hadn't thought about or that I needed to think about more.

Over the years, I've observed David cultivate this dynamic and collaborative approach in each discussion he's a part of, from one-on-one interactions to board meetings. But whatever the setting, David's heart remains the same: to strengthen the organization and its leaders, so that they can serve the Lord and others to the very best of their ability.

About 10 years ago, David introduced me to a promising young leader in the field of Christ-centered international development. Five minutes into the call with Peter Greer, I was blown away by his field experience, education, and intelligence. Over the next several years, as he and I served on several boards together, I noticed what is perhaps his most unique gift: his Colombo-esque manner of asking course-altering questions. Like Colombo, the famous television detective, Peter has a way of humbly posing intelligent and impactful questions. Often a motion is made, a second has been added, and the call for "all in favor to

11

say "aye" is imminent, when Peter will say, "We've discussed many good options, but might we also want to consider...?" This seemingly simple question leads to additional discussion producing a much better outcome. Serving alongside Peter as a board member, I appreciate the way he gets us to take a deeper look at an issue and how his simple yet profound questions move us to a better place.

What I love about this short book is the opportunity for you to "listen in" to some of the conversations and questions from David and Peter about effective board governance. Throughout the course of their lives, serving as CEOs of organizations and as members on many boards, they have lived out the contents of this book. The ideas of this book are not based just on good research but on their own personal experiences.

The subject matter of this book is crucially important. I've read articles and white papers about what makes an effective board and how to be a better CEO, but I've never read anything that specifically focuses on the relationship between the board and the CEO. The irony is that most of us reading this book would agree that having not only the right leadership structure but also the right relationships between leaders are perhaps the most critical factors in the health of any organization. I've seen far too many well-meaning organizations never become what they desired because leaders have not entered vital, working, trust-based relationships with each other. I've seen strong CEOs who don't listen to their boards only later to find themselves at odds with them. Conversely, I've seen promising boards fail to empower their CEO, leaving board members scratching their heads, wondering why they can't find a strong CEO to run the organization.

As you read these pages, there will be some things that will challenge "business-as-usual" thinking and introduce new practices to enhance your governance practices. David and Peter both have the desire for organizations not only to remain centered on their mission, but to thrive, and I am confident—as you apply these principles—that will be the outcome.

I'd invite you to not just process the words of this book, but to take the posture I assume each time I meet with either of these leaders. Allow them to ask the hard questions of you. Allow yourself to engage and grapple. And most of all, allow yourself the freedom to envision a thriving, healthy relationship among the leaders of your organization as you serve and lead, able to do more in your work together than you could ever accomplish on your own.

Tiger Dawson
President of Edify

INTRODUCTION

Surrounded by Revolutionary War battlefields, I (Peter) joined a dozen faith-based nonprofit leaders from across the country for a unique learning experience. Using the methodology of "peer member processing," our two days together would focus on helping each other go to war on the most significant challenges we faced.

In preparation for the experience, we were asked to come with our response to one simple question: What is the most significant obstacle you are currently facing?

In small groups, we would confront these obstacles, with the goal of helping each leader discover a positive resolution, or at least identify a few of the next steps to take.

Driving to the event, I wondered how many would choose to talk about the seemingly impossible task of "balancing" work and family. Or how many would focus on the challenges of fundraising. Maybe strategy would come up. Or operating in a rapidly shifting culture.

But the issue that felt most urgent was my

relationship with my board. We were in a season in which we were facing key decisions and operational dilemmas.

Compounding these challenges was my sense that I was receiving conflicting counsel from several board members. How was I supposed to follow the directions of my "bosses," when one board member's advice sometimes contradicted another's?

Given my deep respect for each board member, and knowing each had the organization's interests in mind, I was confused. There was no question that our *intentions* were all in the right place, but our *practices* were leading to conflict and confusion.

Arriving at the retreat center, the group of nonprofit leaders began sharing their obstacles, and a pattern quickly began to emerge: One after another, leaders shared that their greatest difficulty related to some aspect of their relationship with their board. Turns out, my challenges were not unique.

It quickly became clear that we were each describing variations on the same theme: the board–CEO relationship is *exceptionally* challenging. It's a proverbial minefield, with the potential to sabotage an organization: creating dissention, thwarting progress, undermining impact, and knocking it off mission. And it's not just organizational leaders who acutely feel the challenge associated with this relationship. Board members often grapple with similar issues. Seldom is their relationship with the CEO easy to manage.

However, with the right practices in place, the board and the CEO can engage in a powerful, genuine relationship. Channeled in the right way, their engagement can result in fresh perspectives and new growth rather than perilous pitfalls.

For an organization's health and vitality, there is no more important, or more complex, relationship to navigate.

A few years ago, Rice University invited me (David) to speak to a group of 200 nonprofit board members and CEOs at a conference focused on good governance. Looking around the packed room, I opened with a simple exercise: "Raise your hand if you would like a more engaged, impactful board." Nearly every hand shot up. Board members and CEOs alike.

Clearly, the desire for a healthy, productive board isn't rare—but actually having one seems to be rare. What accounts for this disparity between vision and reality?

As someone who has served as a board member and chair of the board for several organizations, I recalled numerous questions that challenged me in my early years in governance.

How can organizations prevent board distance or disinterest? Is the board chair or the CEO responsible for cultivating board engagement? What qualities make up a great board member? What aspects of organizational leadership and governance fall to the board and which to the CEO?

Discovering the answers to these questions was my first step in developing a more engaged and impactful board, which in turn, helped to foster a stronger relationship with the CEO and led to a better functioning of the organization as a whole.

Indeed, creating a healthy relationship between the board and the CEO not only affects the two entities involved, but flows down to affect staff members, interns, volunteers, and even the clients or beneficiaries that the organization serves.

For an organization to thrive, a healthy board–CEO relationship must be at the center.

What's at Stake?

Getting the board–CEO relationship right is mission-critical. Its importance goes far beyond just trying to mitigate confusion, discover big-picture alignment, or build a healthy leadership culture.

Over the past few years, while researching the causes of mission drift with Chris Horst and Anna Haggard, we concluded that drift is far more prevalent than we might expect. Silently and with little fanfare, organizations routinely wander from their founders' original intent and mission. From Harvard University to Franciscan food banks, strong foundations have eroded over time as new leaders gradually lost sight of their organization's mission. Like a current, drift carries organizations away from their core purpose and identity.[1]

At the center of this organizational drift is often an unstable board–CEO relationship. We have seen too many organizations drift, self-destruct, or shut down as a direct result of missteps in this key relationship.

Our intention in writing this book is that there would be a resurgence of called and equipped leaders who remain on mission, positively impacting our world for decades to come. "In [their] simplest form, Mission True organizations know why they exist and protect their core at all costs. They remain faithful to what they believe God has entrusted them to do. They define what is immutable: their values and purposes, their DNA, their heart and soul."[2] To accomplish that goal, it is essential that leaders successfully navigate the core board–CEO relationship.

Our Story

Our (Peter and David's) friendship began in 2006, and centered initially on the African nation of Rwanda. I (David) had just returned from a trip focused on engaging more intentionally in global philanthropy. Since Peter had just been living there for three years, we connected over what it might look like to impact that nation.

Following that initial conversation, we have traveled together to multiple countries and engaged in many conversations about what it takes to build high-impact organizations.

We chose to write this book together because we realize that the board–CEO relationship is a crucial, yet challenging relationship. Of the small number of books written on the significance of this relationship, very few offer insight from both points of view (an organizational leader and a board member). We believe CEOs and board members are called into relationship with each other and must work together to advance the mission. To that end, throughout this short book, we offer two perspectives we hope will challenge and encourage you to develop strong, vibrant relationships within your organization.

The focus in this small book is exclusively on one facet of governance which is essential for an organization to stay focused on its mission: the board–CEO relationship.[3] Drawing on our personal experience, we hope whether you're a board member or part of a leadership team, you will find this book practical, to-the-point, and encouraging as you seek to lead more effectively.

Before we dive into practices to help make incremental improvements to your board–CEO relationship, here are four quick disclaimers:

First, as people who have worked with us are likely able to attest, we are not perfectly living out the principles in this book. Please know that we are approaching this subject as part of our own learning with the hopes that our successes, failures, and ongoing study might help you more effectively help your organization to stay on mission.

Second, due to requests from friends who generously shared their stories, a small number of names and details have been altered to ensure anonymity.

Third, even though we use the term "CEO" in this book to refer to the organization leader, we recognize that there is a broader range of titles for individuals reporting to a board. In this book, CEO is a broad term which refers to executive directors, presidents, managing directors, pastors, and any other organizational leaders who report directly to a board.

Lastly, much of our experience is serving with faith-based organizations, and our faith is the core of who we are. For Christian organizations, especially, there is so much riding on modeling a healthy board–CEO relationship. This comes from a knowledge that the mission functions, first and foremost, to honor God. If the board–CEO relationship gets off track, there is the possibility that it could discredit the mission. That said, we believe these principles could be applied successfully in a broad range of settings, since a healthy board–CEO relationship is critical for long-term success of any organization.

With the right attitudes, expectations, and actions, the board–CEO relationship can bring renewed vision, health, and vigor to an entire organization. Rather than adversaries, the two parties can become allies in a shared mission. It takes planning, intentionality, and hard work, but it is possible for this key relationship to flourish.

1

MISSION,
NOT EGO

K.P. Yohannan was in his early 20s when he said
goodbye to his family, friends, and Indian homeland and
moved to the United States to pursue a degree in biblical
studies. Just months into his education, Yohannan
became an ordained minister and served as the head
pastor of a Native American Southern Baptist church for
four years. Today, he is globally recognized as the
founder and director of Gospel for Asia (GFA).

As one of the largest international nonprofits in the
world, GFA focuses on the transformation of

communities in Asia through the love and hope of Jesus Christ. They strive to meet the deepest needs of others by providing access to education, healthcare, and disaster relief.

Yohannan's book *Revolution in World Missions* serves as a clarion call to redesign how we think about equipping national leaders to reach their communities for Christ. While I (Peter) was in college, this book had a dramatic impact on shaping my calling and approach to missions.

GFA's impact over the years is unmistakable, positively impacting millions of people throughout Asia. Yet recently, decades of faithful service have been called into question.

According to *Charisma* magazine, the missionary organization "solicited hundreds of millions of dollars for the charity but then misdirected the money to GFA leader K.P. Yohannan."[1] The Evangelical Council for Financial Accountability (ECFA), the premier accreditation agency for faith-based organizations, reported that GFA used nearly $20 million in restricted donations to build a new headquarters. Although the donations were intended for overseas mission work, the GFA's 2013 audit listed the money as an anonymous donation.[2]

After four months of investigating the financial integrity of the organization, the ECFA revoked Gospel for Asia's 36-year membership.[2]

As time wore on, a deeply concerning pattern of regularly concealing information from the board emerged, particularly in relation to the organization's finances. After GFA's expulsion from the ECFA, board member Gayle Erwin recognized the enormity of the controversy and recommended that the GFA leaders publicly apologize. Instead, "he was instructed to write a report that rejected the accusations and vindicated GFA's leaders."[2] Erwin no longer serves on GFA's board.

It took investigative journalism, rather than basic nonprofit governance, to unearth the financial malpractice. Decades of trust eroded in a matter of months. Faithful supporters walked away feeling hurt. Staff felt betrayed. And the organization has spent an exorbitant amount of time and energy attempting to get back on mission.

Our hearts break for the challenges they have experienced, and we believe that it could have been prevented.

While Yohannan and GFA violated many nonprofit best practices, at the core was a board that lost its mandate of effective oversight. The board was unable to keep the organization and its leaders on mission.

At age 22, Robert Robinson penned the hymn "Come Thou Fount of Every Blessing" and included the words, "Prone to wander, Lord I feel it / Prone to leave the God I love." He understood his own heart well enough to know that the seeds of drift are in all of us, and drift is possible for every CEO, every board member, and every organization.

Due to our human propensity to drift, the board and CEO's relationship must center on and routinely return to a shared commitment to the mission. Otherwise, it is too easy for organizations to bend toward the interests and egos of their leaders, instead of toward the people they serve.

When one person, whether it be the CEO or a board member, becomes the focus, the organization becomes a ticking time bomb. Self-centeredness undermines any relationship, and when it runs wild within an organization, it will cause an explosion, releasing shrapnel that can leave irreparable damage.

"When a ministry encounters failure—or even worse, scandal—its difficulties can almost always be traced to a breakdown in governance," states the ECFA. "The importance of an active, informed governing body cannot be overemphasized. Left unchecked, even minor board neglect can eventually intrude upon the accountability and effectiveness of the ministry."[3]

We don't want one more organization to have to go through the challenges GFA has experienced. We don't want one more unhealthy board–CEO relationship to cause organizational mayhem.

Since the original ECFA reports surfaced, Yohannan has apologized for the ministry's failings in a published letter in *Christianity Today,* promising to improve for the future. "To date, we have implemented or are in the process of implementing every one of the changes learned through the ECFA review... We have engaged outside counselors who will help us achieve the level of excellence and accountability our donors deserve."[2] We celebrate the steps GFA is taking to get back on mission, and believe that this could be a key turning point for the organization.

Still, upon hearing about this situation, I (David) was deeply concerned and wondered if there might be organizations that I was actively supporting that might be on a similar track. Would any of the organizations I support make future headlines? I began to wonder how we might ensure that this situation was not repeated, or at minimum, was caught and corrected before it caused such harm.

In assessing an organization, I want to know if the board–CEO relationship is founded on the premise that, together, they share a common mission. This mission must always supersede personal agenda or personal interest, including the personal interest of the founder, CEO, or any member of the board.

It's Bigger Than You

Serving as a board member or the CEO of a nonprofit demands a posture elevating the mission over any one person, and a commitment to the notion that the mission is much bigger than *you*. If you don't have this foundational attitude in place, no systems or dedication to procedures will ever compensate for its lack. With a small group of board members dedicated to holding each other and the CEO accountable and committed to speaking the truth in love, organizations are set up to flourish.

Healthy boards and CEOs must never let personal ego undermine the potential of their organization's impact. They understand that the mission is what matters most.

Mission Over Money

It's not just CEOs who struggle to remember this underlying issue. Phil Clemens is chair of the Hatfield Corporation and an active board member on several for-profit and nonprofit organizations. He observes, "If board members are also significant financial partners, they can fall into the temptation of viewing their donation not as a gift but as if they're buying a share of the organization."

Financial gifts and board membership can lead a nonprofit board member to feel that personal desires and expectations should be prioritized, even when they conflict with the broader mission. Every board member must constantly focus on the organization's core purpose, not their personal preferences.

The goal of the board and CEO is the same: accomplishing the mission. Not prestige. Not perks. Not even the feel-good sensation that comes with serving. The role of a board member or CEO is service. It's not an award and it doesn't come with a gold star, trophy, or merit badge.

In large measure, your contributions may not be seen or fully appreciated, and humility is a starting point for a healthy board–CEO relationship. In fact, the apostle Paul's words are fundamental to this relationship: "Honor one another above yourselves."[4] Nonprofit leadership is hard work, but it comes with the perspective that if done well and with humility, the organization will be able to accomplish its mission more effectively.

What unites the board and CEO is a common commitment to the idea that the flourishing of the organization and achievement of impact are much higher goals than anyone's personal agenda. At the center of thriving organizations is a shared understanding that the mission is what matters most.

THE PRACTICES

- Evaluate your organization's mission statement. Developing a clear, concise mission statement is integral to organizational health and to staying on track. Ensure that your mission statement focuses on what you do, who you do it for, and how or why you do it.

- Some boards open each meeting with a reading of their organization's mission statement, as one small way to bring proper perspective, regularly reorienting each person to the ultimate purpose of their efforts. Others intentionally incorporate impact stories to focus the conversation on the people served.

APPLICATION QUESTIONS

1. How might you as either a CEO or board member identify if your personal agenda is slowly becoming more important than the organization's agenda?

2. How would you deal with a board member or a CEO who seemed to elevate a personal agenda above the organization's objectives?

3. What are some ways that you can intentionally guard the mission of the organization?

2

CLARITY, NOT CONFUSION

Gathering at the Mt. Washington Hotel in picturesque New Hampshire, the board of HOPE International assembled for two days of strategic planning. Sixty years earlier, this hotel had hosted 730 delegates from around the world with the mandate to craft a plan to rebuild the global economy after World War II's devastation. In the very place where we were meeting, agreements were signed in 1944 to create the International Bank for Reconstruction and Development and the International Monetary Fund.

With the backdrop of this historic summit, surely the issues on our agenda would seem insignificant in comparison. We were only a dozen people from one continent, and we were trying to build a nonprofit organization, not rebuild the global economy.

As we gathered, we considered whether it was time to expand geographically, or to go deeper in our existing footprint. Should we begin to offer new services or focus on our existing ones?

Identifying the items to put on the agenda proved easier than finding the solutions. Underlying these discussions was ambiguity about how decisions were made. Ultimately, who made the call? What decision needed a board vote, and what fell within the CEO's responsibilities? What part of the discussion was advice, and what was a binding resolution? What were the roles and responsibilities of the board and CEO?

By the end of the first day, my (Peter's) head was pounding.

Divide and Conquer

Alignment on the overall mission does not guarantee a healthy board–CEO relationship, especially if there is confusion over the specific roles and responsibilities.

For many board members, the question is, "I want

to help, but what exactly am I supposed to do?" Similarly, many CEOs wonder, "I want to engage my board, but what are the rules of engagement and what am I empowered to do without their approval?"

If we don't understand the specific roles and responsibilities of the board and CEO, we are creating a fault line that will eventually send shockwaves through this most important relationship.

The clearer the job description, the easier the job. As *The Nonprofit Board Answer Book* summarizes, "Everyone becomes more productive when board and staff members do not spend time doing one another's work."[1]

In oversimplified terms, the relationship between the board and the CEO might best be described in terms of the relationship between the coach and the quarterback. Both have a shared agenda: win the football game. There is no ambiguity about the goal they pursue. But everyone knows they do not have the same role.

The coach selects the quarterback and creates an overall strategy, but on game day, no matter how involved the coach is on the sidelines, you'll never see him or her step onto the playing field. The coaches can shout, use colorful language, direct the overall plays, and even foam at the mouth, but they never throw a pass. For better or worse, the field is the quarterback's domain.

Similarly, the board functions as the coach. They

select the quarterback (CEO), make a game plan (set overall direction), and then empower that individual to play his or her role. Unless there are dire consequences related to letting the CEO continue in this role, the board does *not* engage in the day-to-day affairs of the organization. If the CEO is consistently not meeting performance expectations, it is time to find a new quarterback![2]

Like this basic analogy, the core roles and responsibilities of the board and the CEO do not need to be overly complex. But they *do* need to be distinct and clear. The following lists are the job descriptions of the board and the CEO, respectively.

The Board's Job Description

1. Protect the Mission.

Keeping the organization on-mission is the board's primary responsibility. Practically, board members set policy, approve budgets, guide strategy, and manage the senior executive, but at their core, they exist to protect the mission and ensure impact. Board members serve as guardians of the mission.

Often, however, board members are foggy or unclear on the mission of the very organization they serve. Phil Clemens estimates that only 10–25 percent of board members have clarity on the overall mission.

He observes, "Boards should know the mission of their organization and do everything possible to ensure the organization stays focused on it. When the opportunity for a new direction comes up, they just need to answer the question, 'Does this fulfill our mission?' And if something outside the mission comes along, even if it's a great thing, it's easy to say 'no' to, because it doesn't fit with the mission."

Because mission drift is such a powerful and destructive force in organizations, the board has an irreplaceable role to identify, clarify, and remain focused on the organizational mission.

2. *Hire and Evaluate the CEO*

John Carver, an expert on board governance and the developer of the Policy Governance Model of leadership, argues that "the most important task of a board is the choice of a CEO."[3] This is one of the explicit and universal functions of *every* board. The board has the ultimate authority to select, empower, and evaluate the organization's chief executive.

Annually, healthy boards walk the CEO through a formal assessment to review performance, set goals for the coming year, and identify areas for improvement. The board is to hold the CEO accountable for results, even when this involves difficult conversations. We'll discuss the importance of these assessments further in Chapter 4.

3. *Ask the Tough Questions*

Several years ago, I (David) joined the board of an organization without doing appropriate research, and discovered that it was a "friends and family" board. They did not hold the CEO accountable, and the board meetings turned out to be nothing more than a social gathering. Not that I didn't enjoy the relationships, but I cared about the mission and wanted the organization to succeed. After a few months of asking questions and digging in, it was apparent that the organization was headed for insolvency. Worse, it didn't seem that anyone wanted to ask the tough questions needed to fix the problem.

Healthy boards ask tough questions, challenge the CEO in constructive ways, and find their social needs met outside of regular board meetings. While strong relationships between board members and the CEO are important, they should not take precedence over addressing hard questions. If they do, it may lead to conflicts of interest and difficulties challenging group decisions—both which taint the decision-making process.

Since the board is accountable for the approval of strategic planning and direction, it is their responsibility to provide oversight on the effectiveness of the organization, including stability and impact. Impact only comes through asking the tough questions and maintaining high expectations. This prevents rubber stamps and pushes an organization forward to achieve its greatest potential.

Self-Managing

It is up to the board themselves to assess how well they are staying focused on these three primary responsibilities. Are they bringing the right people with the right skills to the board, orienting them to their roles and responsibilities, and organizing them in a way that best advances the work of the board? Boards should engage in self-evaluations annually to ensure they are focused on their core responsibilities, and that these responsibilities are performed with focused excellence.

The CEO's Job Description

The CEO is responsible for implementing the mission. While the specific responsibilities vary from organization to organization, this includes building the team, raising resources (with the board's help), and ensuring operational excellence. Though never done alone, the CEO is called to do everything possible to ensure that the mission is fulfilled.

As Carver succinctly puts it, "the CEO is accountable for no less than the entire product and behavior of the organization. That means everything except the board and its functions."[4] No pressure!

Because the role is, in some ways, so expansive and general, there is potential for excess in one of two ways. Carver explains, "Nonprofit and public organizations have chronic problems with the CEO function, because it is either overpowered or underpowered…. Many boards unwittingly invite their CEOs to be either manipulators or Milquetoasts."[5]

The role of CEOs is a sink-or-swim situation. The role often has high visibility, high demands, and high stakes. So, if you are a CEO, put your bathing suit on and get ready to jump in.

Crystal Clarity

A healthy board–CEO relationship thrives on crystal clarity on specific roles and responsibilities. Justin Miller, founder and executive director of CARE for AIDS, recognized the ambiguous roles between the board and CEO as he was growing the organization. Instead of waffling through unnecessary ambiguity, he engaged an external consultant and created a board manual that includes specific language around the roles and responsibilities.

The CARE for AIDS board manual opens with the following quote: "Board leadership requires, above all, that the board provide vision. To do so, the board must first have an adequate vision of its own job. That role is best conceived neither as volunteer-helper nor as watchdog but as trustee-owner."

Many non-profit manuals feature hundreds of pages that tell a CEO what he or she *can* do. However, this creates CEOs who feel stifled and must always seek approval for new initiatives. In turn, these CEOs stop innovating, taking risks, or pursuing ideas beyond the norm.

Justin suggests using manuals that empower a CEO rather than stifle his or her creative freedom. "Instead of declaring what a CEO *can* do, our manual highlights what is *off limits"* he explains. For example, the CEO may need to gain board approval in order to take on debt, lease new property, or make changes to the mission of the organization. Information not covered in the manual is under the CEO's discretion, thus giving him or her power and creativity to lead the organization well.

The board exists to give oversight and direction, not

to run the organization. If the board is confident in their choice of CEO, they will recognize that while they may not agree with the CEO's every decision, they chose the CEO to do the job of running the organization. It is in the organization's best interest to keep the board's and CEO's roles distinct.

Not getting involved in daily affairs also means that the board does not manage staff. Except for an internal audit leader, the CEO is the only staff member who should officially report to the board. Other senior staff may provide periodic updates or reports to the board to give a broader view into the organization, but that is entirely different from the board having many different reporting relationships. When multiple individuals report directly to the board, often that means there are often storm clouds on the horizon.

Healthy delineation and interaction between the three constituencies of an organization—board, CEO, and staff—can be visualized as an hourglass. The top half of the hourglass represents board members and their responsibilities; the bottom half is the staff and the daily affairs of the organization. The narrow neck in the middle of the hourglass—where *all* sand must filter through—is the CEO. Board members, and their expertise and advice, don't bypass the CEO on their way to the other half of the hourglass. Likewise, staff members don't go directly to board members to discuss their daily responsibilities. It is the role of the CEO to bridge this divide. Board and staff may communicate directly on specific issues, as long as the CEO is kept updated and informed.

A massive amount of frustration can be avoided by following this simple framework. It also makes the task of clear communication far simpler. The reason is obvious: there is little ambiguity about overall direction and organizational priorities. When it comes to the board–CEO relationship, there will always be a certain level of ambiguity. But, it's in all of our best interest to avoid any *unnecessary* ambiguity and work to ensure a smooth functioning of the organization.

Getting roles and responsibilities clear is a great starting point to ensure that your organization's hourglass doesn't break. But it's only the beginning.

THE PRACTICES

- Create a board manual, listing internal or external resources to articulate the distinct roles and responsibilities of the board members and of the CEO.

- Clarify which responsibilities require board approval

and which tasks the CEO is empowered to accomplish without the board.

- Distribute the board manual to each board member upon their appointment to the board, and regularly remind board members of its existence. Refer to the manual when questions of roles and responsibilities arise. If new roles and responsibilities surface as the organization grows, add them to the manual and redistribute.

APPLICATION QUESTIONS

1. Does the organization have a list of actions to be approved by the board before implementation? (For example, is there an expenditure limit the CEO can utilize without asking the board for permission?)

2. Does the board have a document articulating their specific roles and responsibilities as distinct from the CEO's?

3

Consistent Communication, Not Mystery

Prior to working at HOPE, I (Peter) worked for a nonprofit serving in east Africa. While there, I hosted Clive Calver, the organization's CEO, in Goma, in the Democratic Republic of Congo. Months earlier, a nearby volcano had erupted, spewing lava through the heart of the city and causing 400,000 men, women, and children to evacuate their homes. The damage was extensive as lava turned into rock, burying the city underneath. The unmistakable scent of sulfur still lingered in the air.

After a long day of surveying the damage and planning our ongoing involvement, Clive and I had dinner together. Fresh on my mind was the pain and chaos that destruction of any kind can cause, so I asked him about what threats can destroy organizations. I was eager to learn from his vast leadership expertise and expected a lesson on responding to unforeseen crises.

To my surprise, Clive responded without hesitation, "Lack of consistent communication between a CEO and board."

Intrigued, I asked what percentage of time he thought that he should spend communicating with his board.

His response: "25 percent."

Given the many other demands of his role, this seemed like an extravagant amount of time—almost an unwise investment. Surely there must be higher priorities than investing into such a small handful of relationships. Couldn't that amount of time have a much greater organizational impact if invested in other aspects of the organization?

Yet, the experienced leader was emphatic. If a CEO doesn't spend time investing in his or her board, there will inevitably be an eruption and it will be just as difficult to fix those challenges as it would be to remove the molten lava that had just swallowed a city.

Clear Communication

Author William H. Whyte once wrote, "The great enemy of communication...is the illusion of it."[1]

Volumes have been written on the importance of communication in every conceivable relationship, from friends and spouses to colleagues and siblings. Communication is crucial for good interactions and progress, yet it's also fraught with the potential for misunderstandings and conflict.

Good communication begins by establishing trust. Of course, it takes time to develop that trust: to understand another person's viewpoint, determine his or her needs, and continually discover ways to help each other. Face-to-face communication works well in laying the foundations for this kind of transparency in relationships. Whereas written communication tends to be brief and succinct, face-to-face contact often encourages more in-depth conversations. Direct verbal communication also helps to provide clarity, since people are apt to interpret written communication more negatively than intended.

Ensuring clear communication with the board needs to be one of the CEO's highest priorities. It's one aspect of leadership that cannot be delegated. Statistics show that "executives who spend 20 percent of their time on board-related activity have high rates of satisfaction with board performance."[2] The correlation is clear, and the results are tangible. But there's nothing easy about effective communication. The assumption that communication will happen as-needed or that all essential topics will be covered in scheduled meetings of the full board is simply not realistic, and it poses a threat for both the organization and the board–CEO relationship.

Cary Paine, president of the Stewardship Foundation, shares that the board should never wonder about what is going on within an organization. Paine supplies his board with an abundance of information and meeting notes. Board members may choose not to read all of it, but they will have access to all of the pertinent information. Better to err on the side of over-communicating than to suffer the consequences of not communicating enough.

From both a board and CEO standpoint, clear and consistent information is vital to organizational health. This includes clearly communicating past failures and future plans. With an understanding of what has worked in the past and the foresight to see ahead, the board is better equipped to do their job.

Indeed, Chris Crane, founder and CEO of Edify.org, notes that the board and the CEO both must acknowledge areas of concern sooner rather than later. The CEO should report significant problems to the board shortly after the problems arise. "An old adage says that the CEO should never surprise his board of directors. One nonprofit CEO I know routinely includes in the board package a section entitled, 'What is working, and what is not.'"

Likewise, the board chair is responsible to inform the CEO of board member concerns about the CEO and to do so in a timely fashion, so that the CEO has an opportunity to respond to the concerns, and take corrective action if necessary.

Communication is too important to simply wing it.

THE PRACTICES

- Schedule a recurring weekly or biweekly meeting (or report) between the CEO and board chair. Ensure that the CEO communicates directly with each board member with regularity.

- Encourage the CEO to participate in every board committee meeting.

- At least monthly, the CEO should send an email to the entire board with an update on strategic plan objectives, as well as brief highlights of successes, challenges, and goals for the month to come.

APPLICATION QUESTIONS

1. What percentage of the CEO's time is spent on maintaining board relationships? If the CEO dedicates less than 20% of his or her time to board-related activity, what activities might be reduced or sacrificed to dedicate more time to the board?

2. What are the regular communication patterns between the CEO and board? Does communication occur too much or too little?

3. Is there a track record of the CEO sharing significant problems with the board chair promptly? Does the board chair promptly share concerns of the board of directors with the CEO?

4

ACCOUNTABILITY, NOT PLATITUDES

In an office overlooking a mountain of evergreen trees, I (Peter) was engaged in a dynamic conversation with several members of a Colorado-based foundation. Our conversation quickly passed through pleasantries and programmatic updates before focusing on governance. The foundation staff wanted to explore board composition, term limits, board member engagement (in terms of both time and finances), and whether there was real accountability with the board.

"Tell us the last time the board shared constructive criticism with you," they asked.

Behind their question, was a desire to see a culture of true accountability. Was mine a board eager to share platitudes, or did it actively engage in the more difficult job of pushing leaders to improve?

My friends in Colorado understood that accountability is an essential part of the board–CEO relationship.

My thoughts immediately jumped to a situation just a few weeks earlier, where the board had challenged me in an area where we consistently fell short of our goals. As the board shared their concerns and critiques with how I was handling the repeated challenges, my spine stiffened and my pride was bruised. However, in retrospect, the board was not only correct in their critique, but they were fulfilling a key aspect of their board role.

Many nonprofit leaders suffer to some degree with people-pleasing, which makes critique an unpleasant part of the board-CEO relationship. But platitudes won't help you achieve desired impact. Good performance requires challenging conversations and real accountability that stretch and challenge a leader.

Embrace Critique

For most leaders, critique is about as much fun as a root canal. But properly understood, critique serves as an opportunity to learn and grow. Leaders averse to critique stunt growth and maturation in their leadership journey. Welcoming critique goes beyond scheduling regular assessments for a CEO, though annual check-ins on performance are essential. A CEO's evaluation should always include a section for identifying areas for improvement, but feedback should also happen as needed, not merely once a year. There is an art to both giving and receiving well-intended, constructive feedback.

In *Better CEO–Board Relations*, Lister and Gabbay advise against delivering sharp critiques unexpectedly in the setting of a CEO's formal evaluation; instead, there should be "a greater level of ongoing candor and spontaneity between boards and their CEOs to ensure that subtle concerns surface promptly, with the right mixture of candor and grace. Such an environment invites and encourages dialogue, assists the CEO in his or her personal development, and leads to early problem resolution."[1]

Create Space for Candor

The goal of a board is to strive continually to fully attain the mission. Disagreement about strategy and implementation is to be expected, and as a diverse set of strong leaders gather to guide an organization, a little friction should be expected. The key question is whether it will be welcomed.

During one of the most difficult times in British history, Prime Minister Winston Churchill created a system to receive the harshest, yet most essential, pieces of feedback:

> Winston Churchill understood the liabilities of his strong personality, and he compensated for them beautifully during the Second World War. … He feared that his towering, charismatic personality might deter bad news from reaching him in its starkest form. So, early in the war, he created an entirely separate department outside the normal chain of command, called the Statistical Office, which had the principal function of feeding him information—continuously updated and completely unfiltered—the most brutal facts of reality.[2]

Knowing how to create a space where a board's unfiltered critique will be expressed is crucial to a CEO getting the feedback he or she needs to lead an organization well.

Collective Accountability, Individual Advice

During one season in which I (Peter) faced operational challenges, several board members offered contradictory pieces of advice. Believing that I reported to each of them, I was doing my best to implement each of their suggestions. But the counsel I received was in conflict, and it was simply impossible to fully pursue the diverging goals each had set for me.

While walking outside our office, I called Tim, one of the board members with significant governance experience, and asked for his help. "How should I respond when I receive conflicting objectives from various board members?" I asked.

His response brought clarity and altered my perspective: "Remember, you don't report to me or to any other individual members of the board. You report to the collective board, which has authority to determine goals and performance metrics only when it is gathered. Approach other one-on-one conversations with board members as though they are serving as an advisor, not as a supervisor."

In moments of ambiguity or disagreement in board members' advice, Tim continued, I should elevate the conversation to the full board level. That way, I could ensure full clarity on outcomes and objectives, instead of trying to implement each board member's competing advice. Ultimately, it is the role of the board chair, not the CEO, to address and reconcile competing opinions and advice of board members.

It would be difficult to overstate the relief that Tim's comments brought to my leadership journey and relationship with the board. That simple conversation showed me how to listen to the advice from each board member without confusing it with a goal for which I would be held accountable. The power of accountability is to the board as a unit, and their binding authority is at play only when they are gathered.

Formal Process

Accountability is a prerequisite for a vibrant and productive board-CEO relationship.

Formally, boards should evaluate the performance of the CEO according to the annual goals set for his or her performance every year. (A sample CEO evaluation form is included in the Appendix.) During end-of-the-year evaluations, avoid abstract discussions about results. Rather, examine achievements in light of the goals agreed upon at the beginning of the year. Doing so will help to clarify what success looks like and, in turn, what accountability looks like.

Some organizations may find it helpful to engage in a CEO 360 Review. This particular review gives management staff and board members the opportunity to provide feedback on the CEO's performance. Evaluations might include questions about a CEO's leadership skills, strategic objectives, and financial priorities. A 360 Review is uniquely beneficial as it evaluates the CEO through insight from many different perspectives.

The Nonprofit Board Answer Book explains the advantages of a having a clear evaluation process in place:

> A planned, thoughtful approach to evaluating the chief executive removes confusion. Determining evaluation criteria for the chief executive enables all members of the board to operate on the same assumptions and have the same expectations about the organization's direction and priorities. In addition, when the board and chief executive agree on their priorities, staff members

usually receive clearer directions for their work and their own performance evaluations.[3]

Without a healthy process in place to regularly assess performance and set goals, frustration and confusion will likely result.

A friend and colleague had been serving as the head of a large global ministry for six years. A new chair had recently been appointed to the ministry's board, but this didn't cause any immediate concern in our friend's mind; over the course of his leadership, the organization had been growing and advancing, with an encouraging new wave of energy and success. Then, during a routine board meeting, he was asked to leave the room. Upon his return to the room, the board released him from his role. Without warning, he suddenly found himself out of a job. And he had no idea that it was coming.

Our friend later commented that if, prior to this, he had received feedback from board members on areas for improvement, he would have gladly accepted it. But in this case, board members weren't willing to have difficult, direct conversations ahead of time, leading them to take dramatic action, which left a ministry reeling.

The ensuing organizational chaos could have been avoided through regular and candid evaluations.

Healthy board-CEO relationships are marked by systems of accountability where encouragement and critique are an integral part of the organizational culture.

THE PRACTICES

- Schedule annual performance assessments for the CEO. Include in this assessment space to assess performance against annual goals and a time for a conversation about areas for improvement.

- Do an annual written performance survey of the board (sample in Appendix) to review board output and performance.

- During board meetings, hold an "executive session," during which the CEO leaves the room. This practice gives board members the space to offer candid feedback on the CEO's performance. Gardner shares, "The benefits of regular executive sessions, when they are conducted in the spirit of a genuine desire to improve board–CEO relations, are well worth the inevitable discomfort."[4]

- After an executive session, assign one board member to share central discussion points with the CEO. The goal is candor in discussions and candor within the board–CEO relationship. If either the board or the CEO is withholding information from the other, there is a sign that trouble is brewing.

APPLICATION QUESTIONS

1. Does your organization have an evaluation system in place for the CEO? Is he or she evaluated on a regular basis?

2. Does the evaluation of the CEO include time to discuss areas of improvement?

3. What structures are in place to encourage board members to share honest and challenging feedback with the CEO?

4. Does the board have regular opportunities to conduct executive sessions for candid feedback and discussion without the CEO present?

5

Healthy Conflict, Not Kumbaya

"All in favor, say 'aye.'"

Like a room full of agreeable pirates, the "ayes" echoed around the room.

The chair raised his eyebrows and looked around. "Anyone opposed?"

Silence.

The motion was passed; there was no going back. The coming weeks were sure to bring challenges and struggles as the newly elected senior pastor enacted the anticipated, and somewhat drastic, changes that he had discussed with the board.

The vice-chair took a deep breath and leaned back in his chair, glad the vote was over. He knew it wasn't going to be easy; change never was. But, he reasoned to himself, at least the new pastor would have the backing of a unanimous board decision to provide a foundation throughout the transition.

Weeks passed and the pastor transitioned into his role leading an uneasy congregation. As the changes took effect, grumblings festered into complaints in the conversations of unhappy individuals. As the criticism worsened, these bitter members went to one of the board members in frustration, demanding to know why he had chosen to vote for a pastor who was on his way to uprooting the foundations of the church.

Taken back, the board member responded defensively that he had *not*, in fact, voted to employ the senior pastor. Word started to get around, and soon the vice-chair was hearing the congregation accuse the board of inaccurately reporting that they had elected the pastor unanimously.

There was nothing for the vice-chair to do but confront the board member. When he asked why he was telling other members that the vote wasn't unanimous, he unashamedly responded that in the boardroom, he didn't cast his vote either way. When it came down to electing the pastor, he didn't vote against him, but he also didn't vote for him.

Conflict avoidance is not a winning strategy for a vibrant board–CEO relationship. It's not a way for organizations to stay on mission.

The boardroom has to be a place of dialogue, vigorous debate, and decision.

Healthy Conflict

Relationships thrive on candid conversation. The board and CEO must be comfortable asking hard questions and communicating honestly and humbly. The board members are not doing their job if they do not ask about and evaluate the CEO's responsibilities. Likewise, the CEO is not performing his or her duties by failing to communicate the issues threatening the institution to the board. Mutual accountability and a team approach are crucial for a successful partnership and a successful organization.

BoardSource compares the board–CEO relationship to marriage, the kind of relationship that "brings together two people with distinct personalities, experiences, preferences, perspectives, operating styles, and decision-making modes."[1] But like marriages, these relationships are rarely devoid of conflict. The board members and CEO are "proven leaders, meaning each also has a healthy dose of self-confidence, vision, energy, and innovative ideas. Put them together, and you're bound to have disagreements."[2] It's essential to know how to address disagreements with healthy conversation instead of frustrating conflict.

A Foundation of Trust and Respect

The work of the board is done inside the boardroom, but the relationships that make the work possible and successful are formed outside of the boardroom. Healthy board–CEO relationships have a solid foundation. To create an atmosphere conducive to this kind of productive honesty, the board must build mutual trust and common experience.

Core to the board–CEO relationship are two key questions: "Do I respect you?" and "Do I trust you?"

If these questions are not answered affirmatively, there will be no strong board–CEO relationship. But when they are in place, the stage is set for healthy debate and greater organizational impact.

Failing to create a foundation of trust and respect can send organizations of any kind reeling. There are times when boards see weaknesses in their CEO and, instead of coming alongside and helping the executive leader, the boards create a workaround. That is, they establish another person in addition to the CEO who also reports to the board. This process of dual-reporting can lead to frustration and confusion. As leadership coach Greg Campbell summarizes, "I'm not saying that dual-reporting relationships don't work; I'm just saying that I've never seen them work."

When trust is present, people readily admit their weaknesses and mistakes, actively seek help and constructive feedback, and deliberately ask for clarification on issues rather than making assumptions. We tell the truth and challenge each other, even when it is hard truth to swallow, because the board and CEO exist to support, uphold, guide, and protect the mission of the organization. What follows is a description of some of the practices that will contribute to a thriving board–CEO dynamic.

Build Relationships

Any relationship requires time to establish and effort to maintain, and the board–CEO relationship is no exception.

It's difficult to build a deep relationship when every interaction is dominated by work-related conversation. David Spickard, president and CEO of Jobs for Life, recalls that during a time of board transition, he and the new board chair got to know each other outside the boardroom: "The chair and I would go for a run together, and that's the way we would meet." David shares that this time spent together strengthened his relationship with the board chair and, in turn, created a more positive dynamic within the board as a whole.

Cary Paine shared that he developed a healthy relationship with his board through frequent meetings with each member. To this day, he meets weekly with the board chair and quarterly with each board member (one-on-one). Beyond regular board meetings, they also have an annual retreat—focusing partly on relationship building and partly on strategic planning. Time together has made an enormous difference in his relationship with the entire board.

The Board Chair and the CEO Relationship

As the leader of the board, the board chair is the board member with the most direct and consistent contact with the CEO. The importance of this role cannot be overstated; this unique position fosters helpful communication between the CEO and the rest of the board. "Board leaders should be deft at creating cohesion among directors and executives, and bridging the formal gulf between them... focusing directors on strategic content without edging into micromanagement," assert Charan, Carey, and Useem.[3]

While this relationship is important to cultivate intentionally, recognizing a non-functioning relationship is also incredibly important. Take for example the relationship between AIG board chair Harvey Golub and CEO Robert Benmosche:

> Each chafed at the other's will, however, and their kinship never gelled. According to Golub, AIG's CEO had reported to the board that their relationship was "ineffective and unsustainable." Benmosche had even threatened to quit after Golub successfully led the board to reject Benmosche's plan to sell one of the company's divisions.... Instead, Golub resigned from the board because of the unworkable association.[4]

Getting the right combination of CEO and board chair can be an enormous asset in terms of facilitating good communication in the boardroom.

Richard L. Crandall, a "seasoned boardroom inhabitant," agrees that the leader of the board "is the ombudsman between the CEO and the board...You have to know how to work well with all the independent personalities in the room. And you have to make sure that anyone who has something to say has the opportunity to do so without being clipped."[5] Because of this responsibility, it is imperative that the board chair and the CEO have a good working relationship to promote the effective functioning of the board.

The Board Members' Relationship

Without healthy relationships between board members, a robust board–CEO relationship is impossible. Ministry Ventures' coach Jon Bennett notes that the board benefits in "unity through diversity" as "a group of people with different experiences, relationships, and ideas comes together to further the mission of one organization."[6] The responsibility to unite the board and strengthen the relationships between individual members lies with the board chair.

While there are many ways to solidify relationships between board members, intentionally investing in each other's personal and professional lives, within board meetings, tends to be especially helpful. Specifically, board meetings might begin with each person sharing a personal and professional update. The board chair may invite members to eat dinner together before or after meetings. This establishes a culture of trust among members, and that culture of trust welcomes and respects board room disagreement in order to reach the best, most thought-out conclusions.

Know When to Cut Ties

Equally important to building relationships is knowing when to remove board members who subvert the productivity of the organization.

I (David) hold a simple belief that if a board member is both overbearing and unwise, then they need to be removed as quickly as possible. Oftentimes, this is difficult if someone has a multi-year first term. For many boards, they might consider staggering terms 1-3-3, meaning a one-year first term to better understand their contributions, followed by up to two additional three-year terms. This process also helps to determine mutual interest and engagement.

It's better to have the discomfort from one transition than the underlying discomfort from having the wrong person in the room. In certain circumstances, all it takes is one ill-suited board member to undermine the entire board–CEO relationship. Although not a decision made or taken lightly, this drastic measure is sometimes necessary for the good of the organization.

According to James E. Nevels, founder and chairman of The Swarthmore Group and a veteran board member, dealing with a disruptive board member is an art form that takes the shape of a three-step process. The board chair begins by initiating a one-on-one interaction: "A private conversation with a disruptive director, starting with the director's strong points, opens an opportunity to reference weak areas requiring improvements." If this private conversation does not produce the desired effect, "A next step is intervention, coaching included," designed for directors who are well-meaning but may still be ignorant of their detraction from the group's productivity. However, if all other attempts have failed, "a third stage calls for the board leader to simply say, 'I'm sorry,' since real improvement has not occurred, 'it may be time for you to opt out.'"[7]

While the authority for board member removal rests with the board itself, dealing with a disruptive board member is ultimately the responsibility of the board chair. Nevels explains: "When the dynamic between a director and management is not going well, it is incumbent on the chair to confirm with other board members that the person is disruptive and enlist their understanding and aid. That consensus gives the [chair] the moral suasion and explicit authority to remedy the situation."[8]

There have been occasions when the board chair thinks that the Board Governance and Nominating Committee should deal with the disruptive board member. However, the board chair must address this issue.

As part of empowering the CEO to do his or her job effectively, the board chair should ensure that each member assists the group in its function instead of detracting from it.

Encourage Dissenting Voices

Finally, productive, healthy conversation does not mean passive feelings or dispassionate communication; boardroom discussion should be engaging. But it is important to read the dynamic in the boardroom and foster a space for positive conversation in the midst of conflicting opinions. This requires participation on all sides; failing to share one's opinion in hopes of avoiding conflict is failing to do one's responsibility as a board member or a CEO.

John Carver notes that "Boards are overly tolerant of members who fail to share their capacities in a way that enhances the deliberative process. It is not enough to have the potential to be a good board member; the potential must be manifested through participation."[9] A board member's job is, at times, to disagree and to argue in a way that produces results.

The key is to find a middle way between expressing

an opinion too forcefully and not sharing one at all. As Gardner says, "The best boards and CEOs function as a synergistic team, but they should also feel comfortable enough to challenge each other when they disagree or have a different perspective on a problem."[10] Being able to express dissent is crucial to a productive conversation and a functioning relationship.

Brian Lewis advises board members and CEOs to remember that "disagreement is not always conflict." With emotional intelligence, both can present opposing ideas in a strong, yet humble manner. In other words, even the most brilliant ideas won't be well-received if the person sharing them lacks humility or an overall understanding of the group's sentiments. Sometimes, asking permission before sharing opposing views ("Can I speak candidly with you?" or "Can I push back on that?") can bring about more meaningful and respectful disagreement by sharing the power with others. When done well, dissent becomes an asset and a sign of health, rather than a sign of disunity.

If the board doesn't organically express challenges and critiques, make sure the board includes voices that will challenge conformity. Boards tend to fall into groupthink, a dynamic occurring when a team sacrifices a healthy decision-making process merely for the sake of agreement or to end the meeting early. To avoid this, Kurt Keilhacker, board chair of Praxis Labs and the

Veritas Forum, suggests, "In board meetings, appoint someone to challenge group decisions and offer dissenting opinions. This not only enables the group to consider multiple options to make the best decision, but it also helps to prepare for potential backlash from stakeholders who express disagreement."

Lewis agrees, noting that healthy boards are filled with optimists *and* skeptics. When boards are comprised of "optimists, idealists, and cheerleaders"—as they often are—a breakdown in governance becomes more likely. Have the courage to build a board where dissenting perspectives are welcomed.

THE PRACTICES

- Schedule regular meetings between the board chair and the CEO to ensure that they are working alongside each other and fully informed.

- Include in a board manual or company policies a process for dealing with a disruptive or counter productive board member.

- Schedule time for social connection in the margins of regular board meetings. For example, make sure there is ample time for a lunch break or that there is a board dinner.

- Appoint a board member to challenge groupthink in each board meeting, ensuring that multiple viewpoints are brought to the discussion.

- Encourage boards to conduct an annual employee survey so that the board can learn early of any significant problems or decline in staff morale. Conducting the survey via an outside agency like Best Christian Workplaces help to ensure employee anonymity.

APPLICATION QUESTIONS

1. Does the CEO spend time outside of board meetings with individual board members?

2. When is the last time you as a board member acknowledged that another board member was right and you were wrong?

3. Is there a strong relationship between the board chair and the CEO?

4. Has anyone on the board ever successfully confronted another board member about their behavior?

5. What specific steps can be taken now to improve communication between the board and the CEO?

6

PREPARED,
NOT PANICKED

When she was 20 years old, Jena Lee Nardella founded a pioneering nonprofit that experienced rapid growth. Gaining national attention, Jena mobilized resources, built a global team, and spoke around the country. As the ministry expanded, she began to consider her own transition and the nonprofit's succession plan.

Jena expressed uncertainty to her board about how much longer she wanted to serve as the executive director, but neither she nor her board developed a clear plan for succession. She admits that she wasn't sure whether she wanted to stay in the organization, change roles, or move on, and—because her communication was ambiguous—the board went into panic mode. Instead of working with Jena on the best way to transition and remain aligned with the mission, the board quickly met and made recommendations without her counsel. They proposed that the COO transition to CEO, while she remain executive director.

But, as Jena worked closely with the COO during the transition phase, she questioned if his skill sets were what the organization needed in its particular stage of growth. Due to the lack of clear communication and the hurried reaction of the board, the decision did not yield the results that she and her board had hoped for.

Growth stalled and after a turbulent period, the board asked Jena to resume her role as CEO. She is currently going through a second transition. The sudden change in leadership caused significant strain not only for her personally but for the ministry as well.

"I had no idea finding a replacement was going to be so difficult," she shared.

Jena's story, unfortunately, is not unique. Very few organizations have prepared the way for a smooth leadership or governance transition. Yet prioritizing these kinds of conversations is a crucial step in ensuring the ongoing, stable functioning of the organization. It's also a key sign that there is a healthy board-CEO relationship in place.

Preparing for Transition

Focusing on succession planning is an integral part of the board's role in safeguarding the mission and making sure the organization outlasts its current CEO. If the organization is run solely by a charismatic leader with no plan for how the organization will continue when he or she leaves, the board and CEO are not taking sufficient steps to make sure the mission of the organization will endure.

"CEO selection is the most important thing a board does," posits J. Larry Tyler, chair emeritus and former president of Tyler & Company.[1] Without preparation and planning, a leader's transition can blindside organizations, creating turmoil, uncertainty, and a lack of clear direction. The board's job is to plan for all contingencies in this regard, which means facing the scenarios no one else even wants to contemplate: the CEO gets hit by a bus or is attacked by a gorilla, the CEO suddenly decides to move to another company or change careers, the CEO must be fired for personal or organizational reasons. Boards and CEOs together bear responsibility to prepare for transition well so that everyone affected—the board, employees, outgoing

CEO, incoming CEO, management, and clients—experiences the transition as a minor blip in the ongoing trajectory of the organization running smoothly.

Since we all know that executive transitions will happen—and not always as a perfectly timed retirement—boards must be prepared for them. Further, great boards will be equipped not only to receive the news of a transition but also to actively lead the organization through it with confidence and order. Not surprisingly, this begins and ends with good communication between the board and CEO.

1. Have the Conversation

Compass Point reports that both boards and CEOs "are still reluctant to talk proactively about succession and just 17 percent of organizations have a documented succession plan."[2]

Certainly, conversations on this topic aren't easy or comfortable. Board members often don't like to face the possibility of disruption brought on by significant change within the organization. CEOs must embrace courage and humility to look beyond one's own tenure.

Even though selecting the CEO is the board's responsibility, governance experts believe that the CEO should be an active participant in the process. Since the CEO is most likely to have a deep knowledge of the role's demands, a clear sense of the organization's direction, and an extensive network of qualified contacts and colleagues, it makes sense that he or she would have helpful and unique insight into next-generation leadership that would be valuable to the board.

As a CEO, I (Peter) know how intimidating it can be to discuss potential replacement candidates. Still, every January, at the request of the board, I send a list of five names to my board chair. These are people who I believe could do my job—and do it incredibly well. Throughout the year, I'm on the lookout internally and externally for people who might be the right ones to take my place. While I have no plans for transition, I actively involve these individuals in the organization so that they might be attractive candidates when it is time for the board to select a new CEO.

Ultimately, the more proactive the communication, the smoother the transition process.

2. *Know What You're Looking for in a CEO*

According to a HireRight study, 26 percent of employers rely on gut instinct when hiring CEOs.[3] Yet, in order to appoint the right CEO for the organization, boards and CEOs must work together to identify the responsibilities and skills necessary for the next-generation leader to succeed.

This includes annually updating a description of the responsibilities of the CEO. Having a current, complete job description is particularly critical if the organization is driven by an especially charismatic or forceful CEO, since their actual skills may be overshadowed by their personality.

Rather than limiting the search to internal candidates who seem like they would be a "good fit," Andrew Garman, associate professor of health systems management at Rush University Medical Center, and J. Larry Tyler recommend designing a metric looking for specific skill sets. For example, a nonprofit organization that works in the developing world may require a CEO to have experience living in the developing world as well as skill in communicating the organization's mission to high-impact donors through speaking events and one-on-one meetings.

Garman and Tyler explain, "… the natural tendency is to think about succession in terms of specific people, rather than skills and talents. But even strong internal candidates will have strengths and limitations, and when 'working backward' from the person to the job, the limitations often get overlooked."[4] No candidate is perfect, but it is important for the board to ensure that prospective candidates' weaknesses are not in areas that are crucial for the organization's performance. Although each organization has its own culture, needs, and priorities, there are some elements that every organization needs to weigh when considering a new CEO.

Most important, all board members must be on the same page. Rachel Weaver, a senior recruitment and retention specialist at HOPE International, recommends, "Boards must have agreement on the purpose of the CEO role, a vision for its growth, and clear expectations of delivery." As board members clarify these things not only with each other but also with the current CEO, the transition process—when it arises—will be much easier.

Be sure that the CEO description is accurate. There have been cases where the board exaggerates the role of the CEO or minimizes serious problems, and the incoming nonprofit leader, in turn, is surprised when the job description doesn't match the role. Inaccurate position descriptions risk the turmoil of a CEO quitting shortly after starting or losing trust in the board.

3. *Know What You're Looking for in a Board Member*

Chris Crane, founder and CEO of Edify.org, has both reported to and served on multiple boards and understands the importance of getting the right board members in place.

While there may be many prospective candidates, Chris believes that only one in ten will be a good fit for the board. "There are a whole host of issues that might keep a board member from offering their very best," he explains. "Over the years, I've slowly put together a list of the top ten most common characteristics among board members, including those who seek to run the organization themselves, those who understand good governance but don't want to make waves, those who focus on doing things as they were done in the past, those who have valuable input but do not have the time, and so on. Only one of the ten profiles represents a healthy and helpful board member."

That 1-in-10 are those who truly excel as board members: They stand up for good governance, are qualified with relevant skills and expertise, will study board materials and research best courses of action, and are vigilant protectors of the organization's mission. (A complete list of Chris's 10 board member profiles is available in the Appendix.)

We don't share these statistics to discourage or to caricature, but rather to highlight just how slim the margins are between those who can serve and those who can serve *well* on a board.

Considering the dramatic impact even one member has on the organization, catching the right people at the right time who offer the right skills and chemistry is crucial.

Even though board members make immense impacts on organizational direction and operations, rarely do organizations invest as much rigor and intentionality in recruiting board members as they do in recruiting key executives. Often the process lacks consistency or even a clear method. Whatever intentionality an organization has in hiring staff, that same process and standard should be followed with board members.

As illustrated in the board member recruitment process included in the appendix, bringing on new board members requires a checklist for skills-based hiring. CEOs might start by working with a team of current board members (or the board chair) to compile a list of key skills needed on the board. Then, they may consider creating a matrix of the skills of each current board member. When reviewing prospective members, note which skills they will bring to the table. If their skills are already well-represented on the board, maybe they're not the right candidate at this time.

Using board term limits, you can also project forward to see which skills you will be looking for in prospective members in one, three, and five years.

Also, be aware that when you appoint a very large donor to the board, other board members may be more hesitant to speak candidly about problems out of fear of donation reductions. The optimum is to appoint donors who can exercise good governance and advance your mission, regardless of the amount of money they donate.

As a board chair, I (David) have noticed that—though effective board members come from all kinds of fields and professions—some of the most helpful board members are general businesspeople with a passion for the organization's mission.

The key principle in board and CEO recruitment is simple: Don't rush. A vacant seat is better than a seat filled by the wrong person. Don't let an arbitrary number inappropriately direct the process. If you wouldn't hire a new entry-level staff member simply because you're impatient to fill a vacant spot, then certainly don't rush to replace a board member or CEO. Rushed recruitment is a recipe for organizational confusion.

To choose the right successor, whether for a board chair or a CEO, there should be clear articulation and consensus on what the organization is looking for in a leader. Healthy organizations have boards and CEOs who are vigilantly searching for people with the qualifications necessary for organizational leadership.

Be sure that a prospective new CEO or board member is passionate about the primary mission of your organization.

4.   *The Art of Retention*

If so much effort goes into recruitment, then it only makes sense to spend time considering how to retain the CEO and board members. Often, this question begins before an individual is even hired. Do the candidate's priorities align with the organization's greatest needs? Is he or she of the highest integrity? Is he or she committed to the mission of the organization? Does the candidate recognize what is expected of him or her? If the answers to any of these questions are unclear, there is decreased likelihood that the candidate will flourish, regardless of his or her intelligence or confidence.

Given the growing turnover rate for CEOs, Scott Miller from Quorum Health Resources notes that the top reasons why CEOs leave their organizations is for professional advancement, personal and family reasons, and dissatisfaction.[5]

Conversely, CEOs stay at their organizations due to community ties and relationships, loyalty to their organization, satisfaction with their position, and compensation. Therefore, it is critical for the board to build a strong relationship with the CEO and to delineate their expectations in advance. While support from the board is important, offering space for the CEO to create and develop ideas empowers him or her as the organizational leader. Finally, engaging the CEO in the culture of the organization helps to create strong community ties—building loyalty to both the people and the overall mission, thereby increasing the retention rate.

5. *Know the Right Time to Exit*

It takes courage and humility for both CEOs and board members to prepare for the moment when they transition—to ensure that, in a way, their absence will not disrupt the mission. It takes even greater humility and self-awareness to recognize when it is time for a change.

In each stage of growth, certain skills are needed to drive an organization forward. Starting a ministry as an entrepreneur differs from the skill set needed to scale an organization that is already established. Similarly, each growth stage of an organization will require different expertise from the board. Considering what the organization needs at a moment in time should drive questions about staff and board transitions.

Too often, society frowns upon CEOs and board members who decide to leave their organization before retirement or the completion of their term. Yet, the leaders who truly honor the mission above self-preservation will recognize when their skills and abilities no longer meet the needs of the organization and when another person's skills may be a better fit.

If the CEO recognizes first that it is time for him or her to make way for a new CEO, ideally the current CEO would provide six to nine months notice to the board of directors. In this way, there is adequate time to find a successor. Staying on for another six to nine months will also communicate to staff, donors, and those outside the organization that there is not an unspoken problem.

For all of us, there will be a time when it will be right for us to transition. Let's not overstay our moment!

5. *Communicate*

As the CEO prepares to exit the organization, communication once again is vital. Ensuring a smooth transition requires dialogue between the board and the CEO regarding the reason for the CEO's departure and the possible internal and external candidates to take his or her position.

The board and the CEO together have a responsibility to develop a plan of how to talk to stakeholders and to create a timeline for the transition process. As the board and the CEO communicate with each other about the leadership shift, it is essential that the CEO corresponds with staff about the transition as well. In short, there should be little to no shock regarding the leadership change.

Not a Big Deal

As the executive vice president and CEO of Martin Limestone Inc., Howard Winey had played a central role in the company's growth. Over his tenure, the organization had expanded to seven additional locations, and after 20 years of service, the time had come for Howard to retire. Fortunately, Howard had worked closely with senior leadership to invest time and energy in preparing for this moment. As a result, in the days, weeks, and months after his departure, everyone—staff, customers, and even Howard himself—was surprised by how little seemed to change. In Howard's own words, "It just wasn't that big of a deal. It had been planned, it had been communicated, it had been prepared, so when it occurred, it was expected and it was good."

Healthy organizations refuse to become dependent on any one person. They build teams with multiple people who are each ready to step up at any moment.

Perhaps part of the reason that CEOs and board members don't actively plan for what comes next is the idea that they are somehow indispensable to the mission. Yet, as mentioned in Chapter 1, it is critical that leaders grapple with the fact that placing ego over the mission inevitably sabotages long-term organizational impact. "Mature leaders hire individuals who are more gifted than they are. They hire people who possess the ability to leverage not only their gifts but also the gifts of others. These people simultaneously build the value of the culture and the organization."[6]

If boards and CEOs care deeply about the mission of their organization, then they will not allow a change in leadership or a change in board members to compromise it.

THE PRACTICES

- Include in the CEO's annual assessment a section for succession planning. Ask the CEO to submit a list of names of individuals that he or she believes could successfully lead the organization.

- Update the CEO's job description annually. Refer to the manual suggested in Chapter 2 to refine the distinction between the board's and the CEO's roles and articulate the tasks critical to the CEO's role.

- Create a list of skills required in a successful CEO candidate for your organization. Refer to this list of skills as well as the growth stage of the organization (rather than the persona of the current CEO) when looking for a successor.

- Create a list of skills and expertise needed on your board. When interviewing candidates, identify whether the prospective board members complement or duplicate other board members' expertise and overall contributions.

APPLICATION QUESTIONS

1. Does your organization have a clear succession plan in place for the CEO?

2. Does the board have a clearly identified list of skills and attributes they will require in the CEO's successor?

3. Have the CEO and the board of directors provided five CEO successor candidates to the Board Governance and Nominating committee?

4. What steps could be taken to improve the board recruitment process?

7

INVOLVED,
NOT DETACHED

In my first few years of getting to know Peter, I (David) sat in on a board meeting for HOPE International. Since these kinds of meetings tend to be the primary place for board activity, I often gauge the vitality and engagement of the board through tracking the conversation. In HOPE's board meeting—like many others that I've attended—I noticed that the CEO spent a significant amount of time talking and leading the discussion. As is often the case when the CEO leads the conversation, the board members become spectators rather than active participants.

Coming out of the meeting, I shared with Peter that, instead of the CEO serving as the primary contributor, the board members should do 80 percent of the talking and CEOs should contribute no more than 20 percent during the meetings. This not only allows for more analysis and objectivity, but it also elevates the conversation.

If a board member during a meeting is crossing the line from staying at the policy level to moving into the day-to-day operating matters, it is the responsibility of the board chair to address and curb that discussion right away. The chair might explain that the issue raised is a management issue, which is left to the CEO's discretion. Instead of discussing the nitty-gritty details of implementation, the meetings allow the board to direct the conversation toward organizational policy and strategy.

Healthy boards adopt the 80-20 method of board conversation. We have seen how this increases board engagement, elevates the conversation, and leads to ownership of the mission.

Deepening Your Board: Ownership

Involving the right people and using the 80-20 rule for

board meeting conversation is only the beginning. I (David) worked with practitioners at a conference to flesh out which factors create an engaged and impactful board, and really, it boiled down to one concept: ownership. Board members must own the highest level strategy questions facing the organization. This ownership comes from feeling accountable for the organization's success.

The CEO, who has the clearest sense of the organization's running day to day, plays a truly unique role when it comes to cultivating this sense of responsibility, both with individual board members and with the board as a collective entity.

Board members that own the mission actively contribute their resources, influence, and expertise to advance the mission.

Resources: Since the board provides strategic direction for the organization, they must ensure that the organization has the necessary resources to carry out that direction. That said, a fully-engaged board requires active participation in fundraising. This calls for each board member to steward their resources wisely.

Jon Bennett, coach of Ministry Ventures, asks, "If the people closest to the vision are not financially supporting it, why would a third party get involved?"[1] Because of their time and energy investment to the board, each board member should consider the organization within their top giving priorities.

Influence: Board members carry significant influence. As it relates to finances, each board member can use their social capital to provide connections to potential patrons. In fact, because networking is a key responsibility of the board, it may be helpful if each member of the board developed a list of five possible donors to support the organization's endeavors financially. Fundraising aside, board members can champion the mission of the organization within their individual spheres of influence—their workplace, neighborhood, and community. This might include knowing and sharing a few statistics or stories with others that reflect the organization's impact in the community and the world.

Expertise: Though board members carry notable influence, they serve on the board primarily for their expertise. On a healthy board, the members represent a range of skills. Members equipped with varied expertise are vital to an organization.

I (Peter) have really appreciated the diversity of skill sets on our board. When HOPE International considered the best way to serve in underserved areas, Andre Mann offered his expertise based on years of working in similar environments. When we tried to figure out how to reach a broader audience, Katelyn Beaty's expertise as an editor of a magazine was instructive. When we needed to strengthen internal controls, Cathi Linch and Jim Deitch brought their CPA and banking expertise to help create stronger systems. At each moment, people with just the right skills and expertise stepped up and offered their wisdom. Certainly, there is a no one-size-fits-all expectation for board members' contributions, but ensuring that the expertise differs among board members is vital for a productive and vibrant board.

When a CEO invites the board into issues of real magnitude, relies upon them to find real solutions, optimistically and transparently works with them, and allows them to have a sense of responsibility for the outcome, boards can reach their fullest potential.

Board Committees

Committees help to define organizational structure and, ultimately, lead to greater board effectiveness. Having a diverse set of committees to employ the knowledge and skill sets of board members spreads out the work of the organization and generates increased board participation. The types of committees often differ from organization to organization. Types may include, but are not limited to, the executive committee, human resources and culture committee, marketing and development committee, programs and finance committee, enterprise risk management committee, audit committee, and the board governance committee.

These committees offer advice based on board members' areas of expertise and provide fuller perspectives on specific aspects of the organization. Oftentimes, this is where the most significant work occurs for board members. Members own the issues and work with the CEO to find solutions to problems facing the organization. This not only includes contributing meaningfully to discussions, but also involves evaluating gathered data, and assessing alternative courses of action.

Maximize Discussion

Since each board member takes ownership on the organization's affairs, maximizing the time to discuss these issues in meetings is vital. At its core, this involves the board chair and CEO working together to create a specific structure: "Meetings that are carefully structured and efficiently conducted will help board members to feel that their time is well spent and that the board adds value to the organization," explains Berit M. Lakey, in *Board Fundamentals*.[2] A structured meeting begins with developing and sending out agendas and materials to each member ahead of time.

Because board meetings occur only a few times each year, the time spent in the meetings is highly valuable. This requires the CEO and each board member to invest themselves fully into the meetings. Michele Ruby, Vice President of Development at The Veritas Forum, notes that many board members simply do not have the time to serve, and this may cause problems for the entire board. "Board members who are too busy to read the reports prior to the meeting, too busy to stay up to date on key initiatives and communications, and too busy to attend fundraising events are all too common." The best boards are those whose members make time to invest productively into discussions by preparing well in advance.

Board members tend to rate meetings highest when there is an agenda directed to strategic issues coupled with plenty of time for interaction and questions. Creating a space for discussion leads to a culture of inquiry. According to *BoardSource*, "a culture of inquiry enables everyone to question assumptions and challenge conclusions in order to reach more complete understandings and make more effective decisions."[3] During times of open brainstorming and general discussion, every person should be heard, even if the chair has to ask more reserved members to participate. This communicates not only the expectation that everyone attends to the discussion and remains engaged, but it also affirms the value of each member.

Effective Engagement

Engaging the board requires both the CEO and the board to work towards a common goal: fulfilling the mission. Even when changes occur in the external environment, the CEO must work with the board to visualize change and encourage continual improvement, while staying true to the organization's mission.

I (Peter) have learned that one of the best ways to reinvigorate passion in board members is to start each meeting with a fresh reminder of why we do what we do. Sometimes, we start with a video or a Skype conversation with one of our global staff members. Recently, HOPE developed a virtual reality tour; so, during one of our board meetings, each member participated in the tour and "visited" the communities where we serve. If possible, board members should be encouraged to witness the tangible results of the mission by visiting areas of the organization's impact. Regardless of the approach, the end goal is the same: to remain engaged in advancing the mission.

THE PRACTICES

- Encourage each board member to share about the organization's mission with at least one person per month.

- Ask each board member to create a list of five potential donors each year for the organization's financial success.

- Send out board meeting agendas and materials 7-14 days ahead of the meeting to give board members enough time to prepare. During the meeting, ensure that each member participates and offers his or her expertise, especially on the subjects that they know the best.

- Schedule 5-10 minutes at the beginning of each board meeting to remind members of the mission through videos, conversations with a staff member or beneficiary, or something else entirely. Be creative!

APPLICATION QUESTIONS

1. Does the CEO spend more than 20 percent of the time talking in board meetings? If so, how do you plan to adjust the system to engage the board in more discussion?

2. What are two practical ways that board members can use their influence to help advance the organization's mission?

3. How can you more fully engage board members in accomplishing the mission?

Conclusion

The board–CEO relationship is like a dance, and there are plenty of examples where a healthy board and a talented CEO end up stepping on each other's feet and awkwardly lurching across the dance floor.

It's not enough to be a great solo CEO, and it's not enough to be a great board if there is not a strong relationship between the two. Boards and CEOs need to learn to dance together.

Brian Lewis summarizes, "The board–CEO relationship can go wrong if the CEO has a low tolerance for ambiguity or is thin-skinned about perceived criticism. From the board side, it can go wrong if board members overstep their role, or otherwise fail to understand it, or if they become too deferential to a leader."

Indeed, this is a difficult dance to master, and perhaps impossible without one final ingredient. As we have seen and experienced, boards and CEOs that stay on mission are united by a deep love for the mission and a deep love for each other.

In 1 Corinthians 13:1-3, Paul writes:

> If I speak in the tongues of men or of angels, but do not have love, I am only a resounding gong or a clanging cymbal. If I have the gift of prophecy and can fathom all mysteries and all knowledge, and if I have a faith that can move mountains, but do not have love, I am nothing. If I give all I possess to the poor and give over my body to hardship that I may boast, but do not have love, I gain nothing.[1]

Love is not a mere surface emotion, rather a brave commitment to put the interests of others above ourselves. To act in ways that actively serve others, even when doing so requires greater patience, flexibility, and self-sacrifice.

We may have abundant resources, hardworking staff members, and even a strong board–CEO relationship, but if we lack love, our organizations will eventually fall apart. They will not stay on mission.

Love creates a culture of honor and grace, which transforms interactions and relationships. It places high esteem on others by encouraging and empowering them to reach their fullest potential. Love refuses to get offended easily, and spends more time growing from criticism than dwelling on it. It does not hold grudges, but is quick to forgive and is intentional about relationship reconciliation.

Focused on the mission and grounded by love, a strong board–CEO relationship will help organizations flourish.

May you lead with a powerful, dedicated love as you build organizations and leave a lasting impact on the world.

ACKNOWLEDGEMENTS

We are grateful for the many friends, colleagues, and mentors who have contributed to this book.

The book would not have happened without Sarah Moon's diligent work and thorough research throughout her summer internship. Brianna Keener spent hours in final research and editing. Both have a very bright future as authors! Additionally, Libby Tewalt, Kristine Frey, Claire Stewart, Ashley Dickens, Dave Wasik, Chris Horst, Julie Heisey, David Lemasters, and Madi Burke all provided constructive criticism and important improvements.

Additionally, this book was shaped through our interviews with Phil Clemens, Justin Miller, Jena Lee Nardella, David Spickard, Howard Winey, Chris Crane, and Peter Teague. Additional insights came through conversations and support from Becca Wammack, Kim Sterling, Charlie Kreider, Michael Bontrager, Cathi Linch, Brian Lewis, Cary Paine, Tim Snow, Dave Blanchard, Eric Thurman, Josh Kwan, and Patty

Dettloff.

This book would not have been possible without the friendship and experiences of so many board members and nonprofit leaders. A special thanks to the HOPE International Board of Directors, and specifically Jeff Rutt, for the continued support of writing projects.

Tiger Dawson has been a mentor and friend for years, and we are grateful for his willingness to provide the foreword.

Lastly, we thank our families, and especially Laurel and Bonnie who beautifully model love and lifelong support.

APPENDIX 1

ANNUAL CEO/ED EVALUATION

*Generously provided by Kim Sterling, founder
and president of Sterling Associates*

1. Please complete the questions below using the following rating scale.

1 - poor
2 - needs improvement
3 - satisfactory
4 - good
5 - outstanding
N - no way to judge

Please feel free to add additional thoughts after each set of choices. The small box provided for these comments will expand to fit your remarks .

1. Board Management

	Poor	Needs improvement	Satisfactory	Good	Outstanding	No way to judge
Relates well to Board Members	○	○	○	○	○	○
Informs Board of objectives, achievements, needs and plans	○	○	○	○	○	○
Works well with Board and staff to implement Board decisions	○	○	○	○	○	○
Provides Board w/solid information and recommendations	○	○	○	○	○	○
Is accessible	○	○	○	○	○	○
Criticizes constructively	○	○	○	○	○	○
Effectively utilizes talents of Board members	○	○	○	○	○	○
Accepts criticism gracefully and productively	○	○	○	○	○	○

Please add any additional comments on how the E.D. manages the Board of Directors

[ ]

2. Community Representative

	Poor	Needs improvement	Satisfactory	Good	Outstandng	Not able to judge
Is an effective communicator	○	○	○	○	○	○
Represents the organization well to the public, is enthusiastic	○	○	○	○	○	○
Develops good relationships with key leaders and donors	○	○	○	○	○	○

Comments on how the E.D. represents the organization in the community

[   ]

3. Administration and Human Resources

	Poor	Needs improvement	Satisfactory	Good	Outstandng	No way to judge
Seeks opinions and ideas of others	○	○	○	○	○	○
Makes decisions effectively	○	○	○	○	○	○
Has good follow through	○	○	○	○	○	○
Establishes priorities for responsibilities	○	○	○	○	○	○
Delegates responsibility and authority	○	○	○	○	○	○
Attracts and retains quality personnel	○	○	○	○	○	○
Demonstrates a good working relationship with personnel	○	○	○	○	○	○
Delivers high quality service to donors directly or w/ staff	○	○	○	○	○	○
Provides regular performance evaluation and counseling of personnel	○	○	○	○	○	○

Any additional comments about admininstrative duties and human resources managment:

[   ]

4 Development/ Fundraising

	Poor	Needs Improvement	Satisfactory	Good	Outstanding	No way to judge
Takes personal ownership of development efforts	○	○	○	○	○	○
Is effective in development calls and group presentations	○	○	○	○	○	○
Follows up leads well and uses Board members effectively	○	○	○	○	○	○
Knows tax laws and implications for charitable giving	○	○	○	○	○	○
Gets results	○	○	○	○	○	○

Comments about Development/ Fundraising:

5. Strategic Leadership

	Poor	Needs Improvement	Satisfactory	Good	Outstanding	No way to judge
Energetically and effectively implements the strategic plan	○	○	○	○	○	○
Assists in development of goals and long range plans Reviews progress towards goals	○	○	○	○	○	○
Gets results	○	○	○	○	○	○

Comments about Strategic Leadership

6. Fiscal Oversight

	Poor	Needs improvement	Satisfactory	Good	Outstanding	No way to judge
Prepares the annual budget	○	○	○	○	○	○
Operates within the limitations of the annual budget	○	○	○	○	○	○
Anticipates and plans for capital needs	○	○	○	○	○	○
Anticipates and plans for cash flow needs	○	○	○	○	○	○
Demonstrates conscientious oversight of School assets	○	○	○	○	○	○
Ensures compliance with relevant government regulations	○	○	○	○	○	○

Comments about fiscal oversight:

7. Please list the E. D.'s Strengths

8. Please list the E. D.'s Weaknesses

Other Comments

Executive Director Evaluation

2. End of Survey

APPENDIX 2

ANNUAL CEO/ED SELF-EVALUATION

Generously provided by Kim Sterling, founder and president of Sterling Associates

Executive Director Self Evaluation

Executive Director Self Evaluation

This is an anonymous and confidential survey that will allow members of the Board of Directors to fulfill one of the Board's most important responsibilities: reviewing, providing feedback to, and supporting the Executive Director. Your name is requested at the beginning for the purpose of tracking participation only.

Please evaluate our Executive Director's performance to the best of your ability using the following rating scale.

1 - poor
2 - needs improvement
3 - satisfactory
4 - good
5 - outstanding
N - no way to judge

Please feel free to add additional thoughts after each set of choices. The small box provided for these comments will expand to fit your remarks .

* 1 Your Name

2. Program development and administration

	Poor	Needs improvement	Satisfactory	Good	Outstanding	No way to judge
Assists the Board in developing, implementing, and evaluating our long-range strategy	○	○	○	○	○	○
Provides leadership in developing programatic and financial plans with the Board of Directors and staff	○	○	○	○	○	○
Assures consistent delivery of high quality programs and services by providing leadership and appropriate oversight	○	○	○	○	○	○
Supervises the maintenance of official records and documents	○	○	○	○	○	○
Ensures compliance with federal, state and local regulations	○	○	○	○	○	○
Maintains a working knowledge of significant developments and trends in our sector	○	○	○	○	○	○
Remains knowledgeable and engaged in fundraising developments and practices	○	○	○	○	○	○

3. Please add any additional comments on how the Executive Director develops and administers programs.

>

4. Communications

	Poor	Needs improvement	Satisfactory	Good	Outstanding	No way to judge
Keeps the Board informed of the financial and programmatic condition of the organization and all important factors influencing it	○	○	○	○	○	○
Is an effective communicator	○	○	○	○	○	○
Represents the organization well to the public, and is enthusiastic	○	○	○	○	○	○
Develops good relationships with key community and civic leaders, associations and donors	○	○	○	○	○	○

5. Please add any additional comments on how the Executive Director manages communications and serves as the organization's spokesperson.

>

6. Budget and finance

	Poor	Needs improvement	Satisfactory	Good	Outstanding	Not able to judge
Develops and maintains sound financial practices	○	○	○	○	○	○
Works with the staff, Finance Committee, and the Board to prepare the annual budget	○	○	○	○	○	○
Operates within the limitations of the annual budget	○	○	○	○	○	○
Anticipates and plans for capital needs	○	○	○	○	○	○
Anticipates and plans for cash flow needs	○	○	○	○	○	○
Demonstrates conscientious oversight of clinic assets	○	○	○	○	○	○
Ensures compliance with relevant government regulations	○	○	○	○	○	○

7. Comments on how the Executive Director manages the budget and finances

8. Administration and Human Resources

	Poor	Needs improvement	Satisfactory	Good	Outstanding	No way to judge
Seeks opinions and ideas of others	○	○	○	○	○	○
Makes decisions effectively	○	○	○	○	○	○
Has good follow through	○	○	○	○	○	○
Establishes priorities for responsibilities	○	○	○	○	○	○
Delegates responsibility and authority	○	○	○	○	○	○
Attracts and retains quality personnel	○	○	○	○	○	○
Demonstrates a good working relationship with personnel	○	○	○	○	○	○
Delivers high quality service to donors directly or w/ staff	○	○	○	○	○	○
Provides regular performance evaluation and counseling of personnel	○	○	○	○	○	○

9. Any additional comments about admininstrative duties and human resources managment:

111

10. Development/ Fundraising

	Poor	Needs improvement	Satisfactory	Good	Outstanding	No way to judge
Develops an annual fundraising plan and oversees its implementation	○	○	○	○	○	○
Is effective in development calls and group presentations	○	○	○	○	○	○
Follows up leads well and calls upon Board members to tap their relationships and experience effectively	○	○	○	○	○	○
Is the main contact for major donors	○	○	○	○	○	○
Knows tax laws and implications for charitable giving	○	○	○	○	○	○
Gets results	○	○	○	○	○	○

11. Comments about Development/ Fundraising:

12. Board Support

	Poor	Needs improvement	Satisfactory	Good	Outstanding	No way to judge
Schedules and organizes agendas for Board meetings	○	○	○	○	○	○
Oversees the preparation of materials for Board meetings, and distributes them to members ahead of time	○	○	○	○	○	○
Assures that the the minutes of Board meetings are recorded and prepared for the Secretary's review	○	○	○	○	○	○
Maintains Board records	○	○	○	○	○	○
Encourages active and effective participation of Board members	○	○	○	○	○	○

13. Comments about Board support

14. Please list the Executive Director's strengths.

15. Please list the Executive Director's weaknesses and areas where s/he could grow or become more effective.

[ ]

16. Other Comments

[ ]

Executive Director Self Evaluation

End of Survey

Thank you so much for completing this survey.

APPENDIX 3

ANNUAL BOARD SELF-EVALUATION

Generously provided by Kim Sterling, founder and president of Sterling Associates

2016 Board of Directors Self-Evaluation Survey

Thank you for completing this confidential Board survey.

An annual self-evaluation is a best practice of effective nonprofit Boards of Directors, allowing Board members to identify strengths and areas of opportunity for improvement. For this reason, we hope that you will dedicate just 10 minutes to complete this short survey, the results of which will be shared in a report to the Board.

The survey results will be collected and analyzed by an independent third party. Your responses are confidential, so please be candid.

To begin the survey, click "Next" below. Thank you!

2016 Board of Directors Self-Evaluation Survey

PERFORMANCE

1. Mission and Vision

	Strongly disagree	Disagree	Agree	Strongly agree	Unable to judge
The mission statement clearly articulates who our organization is, why we exist, and what we do.	○	○	○	○	○
Our mission drives the organization's strategies and policies.	○	○	○	○	○
The Board uses metrics drawn from the mission to assess our organization's performance.	○	○	○	○	○

2. Partnership with the Staff

	Strongly disagree	Disagree	Agree	Strongly agree	Unable to judge
The Board conducts a fair and objective review of the Executive Director's performance on an annual basis.	○	○	○	○	○
The Board ensures that the Executive Director has the authority to make operational decisions for the organization (e.g. hiring and managing staff, managing day-to-day operations).	○	○	○	○	○
Board members refrain from attempting to direct the work of staff.	○	○	○	○	○

3. Fiscal oversight and responsibility

	Strongly disagree	Disagree	Agree	Strongly agree	Unable to judge
100% of Board members contribute financially to the organization	○	○	○	○	○
The Board ensures that the organization has the infrastructure it needs to meet goals (e.g. adequate staffing and facilities).	○	○	○	○	○
The Board sets priorities and monitors progress against financial goals	○	○	○	○	○
The Board ensures adequate risk management	○	○	○	○	○

4. How can the Board improve in the above areas?

2016 Board of Directors Self-Evaluation Survey

EFFECTIVENESS

5. Effective nonprofit Boards draw on best practices to work effectively. Please rate the performance of our Board in these essential areas:

	Strongly disagree	Disagree	Agree	Strongly agree	Unable to judge
The size of the Board is appropriate.	○	○	○	○	○
The Board's composition reflects the diversity of background, expertise, and other resources needed by the organization.	○	○	○	○	○
The Board has effective processes for identifying, cultivating, and integrating new Board members.	○	○	○	○	○
The right leaders are in place as Board chair and committee chairs.	○	○	○	○	○
The Board has appropriate committees with clear charters.	○	○	○	○	○
Expectations of Board members are clearly defined and communicated.	○	○	○	○	○
The Board receives the appropriate materials from the staff in advance of meetings.	○	○	○	○	○
Board meetings focus on key strategic issues.	○	○	○	○	○
Board and committee meetings are run efficiently and effectively (e.g. start and end on time and ensure all voices are heard).	○	○	○	○	○
Board members are provided with many opportunities to participate in board work that connects them to the mission.	○	○	○	○	○

6. How can the Board and the executive team improve in the above areas?

2016 Board of Directors Self-Evaluation Survey

OTHER QUESTIONS

7. What are this organization's greatest strengths? (Consider all areas: staff, governance, programs, facilities, funding, operations, communications, collaborative relationships, etc.)

8. What are this organization's greatest opportunities/needs/challenges? (Again, consider all areas: staff, governance, programs, facilities, funding, operations, communications, collaborative relationships, etc.)

9. How many years have you served on this Board of Directors?

○ 1 year or less

○ 2-3 years

○ 4-5 years

○ 6-9 years

○ 10 years or longer

10. On how many other nonprofit boards do you serve, in addition to this one?

○ No other boards

○ 1 other board

○ 2 other boards

○ 3 or more other boards

11. What skills and expertise do you bring to the Board? (check any that apply)

- [ ] Marketing and communications
- [ ] Fundraising
- [ ] Legal
- [ ] Finance
- [ ] Governance and organization
- [ ] Program
- [ ] Human resources
- [ ] Facilities
- [ ] Board development
- [ ] Partnership strategy

Other (please specify)

12. Where does this organization rank among the charitable causes you support?

- ( ) It's my #1 charitable interest
- ( ) It's in the top three on the list of causes I support
- ( ) It's on my list, but not a priority.
- ( ) It is not one of my charitable interests

Please share additional thoughts, if appropriate

13. Please share anything that the organization might do better or differently to support you in serving as a member of the Board.

14. Please comment on the frequency, length and location of board meetings.

	Agree	Disagree
The Board meets too often.	○	○
The Board doesn't meet often enough	○	○
The Board meets with just the right frequency	○	○
The location of our Board meetings is convenient for me	○	○
Our Board meetings are too long.	○	○
Our Board meetings are too short.	○	○
The length/duration of our Board meetings is just right.	○	○

Other comments about Board meetings?

15. What other feedback and suggestions would you like to share?

* 16. The results of this survey will be analyzed by Sterling Associates. The information you have shared will remain entirely confidential. We are requesting your name only to keep track of participation, and your individual responses will not be attributed to you.

Your name:

2016 Board of Directors Self-Evaluation Survey

Thank You!

SAMPLE BOARD OF DIRECTORS SURVEY

Regarding Your Board Service

1. What are the best and most challenging parts of being on the board? Are you learning? Are you having any fun? Are you contributing?

2. What do you believe is your most significant contribution to the mission?

3. Do you feel like you understand what your "job description" is on the board?
   - ☐ Don't Understand
   - ☐ Somewhat Understand
   - ☐ Mostly Understand
   - ☐ Well Understand

Additional comments:

4. Do you feel like your current responsibilities (as a subcommittee member, board member, or on any "special assignments") take advantage of your gifts and experience?
    ☐ Takes Little Advantage
    ☐ Takes Slight Advantage
    ☐ Takes Good Advantage
    ☐ Takes Full Advantage

Do you want to adjust your responsibilities in any way?

5. Do we communicate well? Are you comfortable with the frequency and level of communication between the CEO and the board?
    ☐ Uncomfortable
    ☐ Less Comfortable
    ☐ Mostly Comfortable
    ☐ Very Comfortable

Additional comments:

6. Are we a high-functioning board? Do you have any concerns on how we function as a board?
   ☐ Low Functioning
   ☐ Less Functioning
   ☐ More Functioning
   ☐ High Functioning

   Additional comments:

7. What pleases you most about our mission?

8. What concerns you most?

9. Are you comfortable with the present direction?
   ☐ Uncomfortable
   ☐ Less Comfortable
   ☐ Mostly Comfortable
   ☐ Very Comfortable

   Additional comments:

10. What will we need more of if it is to have the deepest possible impact on the places where it is working?

APPENDIX 5

BOARD NOMINATION FORM

- A prospective board member must be nominated by an existing board member.
- The nominating board member will fill out a nomination form, which will include a statement making the case for the recommendation of the prospective board member.
- The nominating member must submit a bio, the nominating form, and the recommendation to the board development and governance subcommittee for consideration.
- The board development and governance subcommittee then researches candidates and evaluates their fit with the board's needs and mission.
- The subcommittee brings the nomination to the entire board of directors for a vote (voting may be done either at the board meeting or via conference call).
- If voted in, the board development and governance subcommittee extends an invitation to the prospective Board member.

Prospective Board Member Information

Name:	
Mailing Address:	
City/State/Zip:	
Country (if not USA)	
Work Phone:	
Cell Phone:	
E-Mail:	
If married, Name of Spouse:	
If children, Name(s) of Children and Year(s) Born:	
Home Church (Name/Location):	
Profession/Title	
Employer (Name/Location):	

Prospective Board Member's Areas of Expertise

AREA OF EXPERTISE		NOTES
Audit/Risk	☐	
Banking	☐	
Board Governance	☐	
Donor Network	☐	
Developing Countries (please specify)	☐	

Entrepreneurial Experience	☐	
Discipleship	☐	
Financial Expertise	☐	
IT Experience	☐	
Legal	☐	
Major Donor Fundraising	☐	
Mass Market Fundraising	☐	
Public Relations	☐	
Strategic Planning	☐	
Training	☐	

Other skill sets that the prospective Board Member has that you feel would be valuable:

Reasons for Recommendation

Describe your relationship with the prospective board member.

Why do you believe the prospective board member would be a good fit with the mission?

On which board subcommittee do you think the prospective board member would be able to most effectively serve and why?

What has been the candidate's commitment to our mission?

Please complete this document and return to the Governance Committee Chair

APPENDIX 6

ANNUAL BOARD MEMBER AFFIRMATION STATEMENT

*Generously provided by Peter Teague,
president of Lancaster Bible College*

(Please thoughtfully consider, sign, and return.)

1. I continue to support the mission, vision, values, and leadership of [Organization Name].
2. I understand that board membership requires [Annual Time Commitment] per year of my time, including preparation and meetings. I am able to give that time during the coming [Time Period] and expect to attend all board meetings and committee meetings, unless I give the respective chairman advance notice of my need to be absent for good cause.
3. I intend to contribute financially to [Organization Name] during the year and will help open doors to friends who may be interested in contributing.
4. I intend to attend and encourage others to attend [Organization Name] events throughout the year as my time allows.
5. I have reviewed, signed, and intend to comply with our board's Conflict of Interest Policy.

6. I have reviewed, signed, and am in agreement with the Statement of Faith of [Organization Name].

7. If anything should occur during the year that would hinder me from fulfilling these intentions of being a positive contributor to our Board of Trustees, I will take the initiative to talk with the officers about a voluntary resignation to allow another to serve who is able to meet these shared expectations of all board members.

☐ I am able to affirm all of the above items and look forward to continued service.

☐ Given my current circumstances, I am unable to affirm all of the above and request that the Board of Trustees accept my resignation effective _____ and seek a replacement who can meet all expectations of board members.

_____   _____

Signature   Date

_____

Printed Name

10 NONPROFIT BOARD MEMBER PROFILES

Generously provided by Chris Crane,
founder and CEO of Edify.org

1. **Those who wish to be on the board primarily to have a feel-good experience and to build their resume.** These board members do not wish to hear any bad news and simply want everything to go smoothly with minimal work required.

2. **Those who want to run the organization.** They sense that the organization's problems involve mismanagement and inappropriately cross the line into interfering with the day-to-day activities.

3. **Those who are single-issue focused.** They direct all of their energies to one issue, often at the expense of achieving the overall mission of the organization.

4. **Those who are sincere but inexperienced.** These board members may grow to become contributing members but currently do not know the best practices of board governance and can unwittingly hinder the board's work.

5. **Those who are seeking prestige or an ego boost.** Forceful personalities who are good at political maneuvers push the board in the direction they wish with little regard for good governance or the mission

of the organization. They may also be looking to build their resume of involvements.

6. **Those who understand good governance but do not wish to make waves.** These members will not speak up when the board is being led awry.

7. **Those who are simply unqualified to be on the board.** Often, these members are selected because they are generous supporters, add diversity, or have allegiances to other board members that compromise their fair-mindedness.

8. **Those who are hanging on.** These board members joined the board more than 10, 20, or 30 years ago, before there were term limits. They may have little interest in or contributions to the board, and may be focused on how things were done in the past rather than looking forward.

9. **Those who understand good governance but don't have the time.** While they have much to give, these board members lack the time or energy to be highly diligent in studying board materials and researching the best courses of action.

10. **Those who truly offer the full package.** These board members understand and promote good governance, are qualified with relevant skills and expertise, will study board materials and research best courses of action, will make the hard decisions when necessary, and are vigilant protectors of the organization's mission at heart.

ANNOTATED BIBLIOGRAPHY

Special thanks to Sarah Moon for creating the following annotated bibliography of board resources.

CALLED TO SERVE

Written in letter format from an experienced board member, Max De Pree, to a theoretical less-experienced board member, this book is designed to be a reminder rather than handbook concerning how boards and board members work best. Topics cover the marks and work of an effective board, chairperson roles and responsibilities, and board structure and design.

THE FUNDRAISING HABITS OF SUPREMELY SUCCESSFUL BOARDS

Jerold Panas delivers what is advertised in this incredibly quick and easy read ("A 59-Minute Guide" according to the cover) providing 25 habits of boards with fundraising success. Chapters are 2-3 pages long and involve an anecdote followed by a quick insight before diving immediately into the next chapter. It is easily understood, and full of practical insights. The body of the book is accompanied by a 'Board Member's

Report Card' as a self-evaluation with a scoring rubric to give a quick assessment of board performance.

FORCES FOR GOOD

Forces for Good is a book of the six practices of high-impact nonprofits derived from incredibly sophisticated qualitative research of 12 carefully identified high-impact nonprofits, effectively pioneering the approach to evaluating the effect of non-profit organizations. The book offers as a corollary structure six myths of nonprofit management. The six practices lauded by Grant and Crutchfield are: advocate and serve, make markets work, inspire evangelists, nurture nonprofit networks, master the art of adaptation, and share leadership. Measuring impact for nonprofits is particularly difficult, they note, because of the difficulty of universally evaluating impact where each organization has a different definition of *impact*.

Perhaps the most impressive aspect of this book is its detailed appendices with a comprehensive explanation of the four-phase research methodology behind their findings. Other appendices include a list of field experts in various categories of expertise, case study research guidelines and questions, key stakeholders interview list, and profiles of the case study organizations.

BOARDS THAT MAKE A DIFFERENCE

As *the* founder of the Policy Governance model, John

Carver is the expert in a self-created field of governance writing articles for departments and magazines, holding hundreds of conferences and workshops, and working with thousands of individual boards across the globe. While he presumes that the typical board is grossly underperforming, he also assumes that this can be rectified and that boards can rise to an unprecedented level of excellence in management skills. Although the second edition is nearing its 20 year anniversary in 2017, the insights that rang true in the 1990 version still proved valuable 7 years later as the Policy Governance model gained repute and acceptance across the world. The original ideas behind the Policy Governance model are outlined in this book. This book helps to refocus boards to make sure they're doing *their* job, not the CEO's job or the staff's job. The multiple Appendices provide further explication of applications for governance, bylaws, and policy contributors, and a variety of sample policies placed throughout the book vary from relationship and limitations policies to executive performance and job descriptions policies.

THE NONPROFIT BOARD ANSWER BOOK

The 20th anniversary edition of this book is not outdated because of its age; if anything, the insights designed in the question-and-answer format are more carefully formed and precisely considered because they have been time-tested. Divided into seven parts, the 80 questions cover everything from Basic Board Functions to Selection and Development of Board Members to

Board-Staff Relations. This book is excellent to keep as a reference and serves by providing general advice as well as Suggested Action Steps at the end of each chapter to provide a tangible way to implement the advice in each answer. Armed with various checklists, example forms, worksheets and lists, this book does have a practical application aspect to complement the conversational style of simple questions and answers.

BETTER CEO-BOARD RELATIONS

This book is another short, practical guide to proper organizational functioning that focuses on CEO-board relations and is broken into the following categories: CEO recruitment, communication, CEO leadership, the board chair and the CEO, and executive compensation. Each has selections from essays that have appeared in *Trustee* magazine selected by Karen Gardner (editor) and placed in their most relevant sections. One can find everything from checklists to diagrams to alliterative acronyms to organized plans to sets of questions. Filled with the practical knowledge that can be implemented by and applied to various organizations, its focus is to improve, not create, organizational infrastructure.

BOARDS THAT LEAD

This book has thorough research, primarily in narrative format, filtered through decades of combined wisdom and experience from the collective minds of the writers. In *Boards That Lead*, Charan, Carey, and Useem paint the picture of effective boards and board leadership; they also paint the picture of failed board leadership that resulted in organizational downfall. It is a lengthier read, and takes more effort to effectively engage with the director's checklists, the primary resource for those looking for practical points of application.

THE BOARD-SAVVY CEO

Doug Eadie gives a short, well-written and focused book on the hats a CEO must wear to forge successful relationships with the board and board chair of an organization. The three roles he distinguishes for CEOs to play – Chief Board Capacity Builder, Chief Governing Process Designer, and Chief Governing Relationship Manager – each occupy one chapter of the book after the first chapter, which gives a general description of the theoretical CEO with ideal board report. Each chapter is an even blend of theory, example, and practical application. The book is wise, thorough, and delivers exactly what it promises without being overambitious. It can either be read in one sitting or easily divided into a chapter or two at a time.

NOTES

Introduction
[1] Peter Greer and Chris Horst, *Mission Drift* (Bloomington: Bethany House, 2014), 15.

[2] Greer and Horst, *Mission Drift*, 27.

[3] Since this book is not intended to be a comprehensive guide on governance, we include an annotated bibliography on the broader discussion of effective governance.

Chapter 1: Mission, Not Ego
[1] Jessilyn Justice, "Gospel for Asia Responds to Claims of 'Egregious Abuse,'" *Charisma News,* February 15, 2016, http://www.charismanews.com/world/55166-gospel-for-asia-responds-to-claims-of-egregious-abuse.

[2] Bob Smietana, "Report Details Why Gospel for Asia Lost ECFA Membership." *Christianity Today,* December 11, 2015, http://www.christianitytoday.com/ct/2015/december-web-only/report-details-why-gospel-for-asia-lost-ecfa-membership.html.

[3] "ECFA Standard 2—Governance," last modified 2017, www.ecfa.org/Content/Comment2.

[4] Rom 12:10 NIV

Chapter 2: Clarity, Not Confusion
[1] Berit M. Lakey, *Board Fundamentals: Understanding Roles in Nonprofit* Governance (Washington D.C.: BoardSource, 2010), 254.

[2] HOPE intern, Sarah Moon, is credited with this analogy.

[3] John Carver, *Boards That Make a Difference: A New Design for Leadership in Nonprofit and Public Organizations* (San Francisco: Jossey-Bass, 2006), 153.

[4] Ibid, 159.
[5] Ibid, 154.

Chapter 3: Consistent Communication, Not Mystery
[1]William H. Whyte, "Is Anybody Listening?" *Fortune,* September 1950, 174.
[2] Maria Cornelius, Rick Moyers, and Jeanne Bell, *Daring to Lead 2011: A National Study of Executive Director Leadership* (San Francisco: CompassPoint Nonprofit Services and the Meyer Foundation, 2011), 11.

Chapter 4: Accountability, Not Platitudes
[1] Eric D. Lister and Carolyn Jacoby Gabbay, "Executive Sessions as Standard Operating Procedure," in *Better CEO-Board Relations: Practical Advice for a Successful Partnership*, ed. Karen Gardner (AHA Press, 2007), 53.
[2] Jim Collins, *Good to Great: Why Some Companies Make the Leap and Others Don't* (HarperCollins, 2011), 73.
[3] BoardSource, *The Nonprofit Board Answer Book: A Practical Guide for Board Members and Chief Executives* (San Francisco: Jossey-Bass, 2012), 242-243.
[4] Lister and Gabbay, "Executive Sessions," 55.

Chapter 5: Healthy Conflict, Not Kumbaya
[1] BoardSource, *The Nonprofit Board Answer Book*, 75.
[2] Ibid.
[3] Ram Charan, Dennis Carey, and Michael Useem, *Boards That Lead* (Boston: Harvard Business School Publishing, 2014), 87.
[4] Ibid.
[5] Ibid, 86.
[6] Jon Bennett, *Help! I'm a Board Member* (Ministry Ventures), 18.

[7] Charan, Carey, Useem, *Boards That Lead,* 65.

[8] Ibid.

[9] Carver, *Boards That Make a Difference*, 204.

[10] Lister and Gabbay, *Better CEO-Board Relations*, xi.

Chapter 6: Prepared, Not Panicked

[1] Laurie Larson, "Your CEO: Are You Short-staffed or Shortsighted?" In *Better CEO-Board Relations*, ed. Karen Gardner, 76.

[2] Cornelius, Moyers, and Bell, *Daring to Lead,* 3,

[3] "4 Tips for Selecting a Potent CEO," last modified October 30, 2014, https://www.recruiter.com/i/4-tips-for-selecting-a-potent-ceo/.

[4] Andrew N. Garman and J. Larry Tyler, "What Kind of CEO Will Your Hospital Need Next?" *Better CEO-Board Relations*, ed. Karen Gardner, 3–4.

[5] Scott Miller, *Recruiting and Retaining a Great CEO* (Brentwood: Quorum Learning Institute), 12.

[6] "The Five Attributes: Essentials of Hiring for Christian Organizations," last modified October 20, 2015, http://blog.bcwinstitute.org/bcwi-bookshelf-the-five-attributes-essentials-of-hiring-for-christian-organizations/

Chapter 7: Involved, Not Detached

[1] Jon Bennett, *Help,* 26.

[2] Berit M. Lakey, *Board Fundamentals,* 58.

[3] Ibid, 59.

Conclusion

[1] 1 Cor 13:1-3 NIV

ABOUT THE AUTHORS

Peter Greer

Peter Greer is President and CEO of HOPE International, a global Christ-centered microenterprise development organization serving throughout Africa, Asia, Latin America, and Eastern Europe. Before beginning his role at HOPE, Peter worked as a microfinance practitioner in Cambodia, Zimbabwe, and Rwanda and earned a master's degree from Harvard University. He has co-authored 10 books, including *Mission Drift*, *The Spiritual Danger of Doing Good*, and *Created to Flourish.* Peter and his wife, Laurel, live in Lancaster, PA, with their three children. peterkgreer.com

David Weekley

David Weekley is the founder of one of America's largest private homebuilding companies, ranked the #14 Best Company to Work For by *Fortune* magazine in 2015. As a community leader in Houston, Texas, David has served on over twenty local boards involved in healthcare, education, and character development. Through the David Weekley Family Foundation, he's worked closely with dozens of global non-profits, including International Justice Mission and HOPE International. In 2015, he was awarded the William E. Simon Prize by Philanthropy Roundtable. David and Bonnie have been married since 1976 and enjoy spending time with their children and grandchildren. They reside in Houston, Texas.

ABOUT THE ORGANIZATIONS

HOPE International

HOPE International invests in the dreams of families in the world's underserved communities as we proclaim and live the Gospel. We provide discipleship, biblically based training, savings services, and small loans, empowering women and men to use the skills God has placed in their hands to provide for their families and strengthen their communities. For specific resources on HOPE International's approach to spiritual integration, operations, fundraising, governance, and more, visit www.hopeinternational.org/resources.

David Weekley Family Foundation

The David Weekley Family Foundation strives to engage the world with integrity, creativity, curiosity, faith, and gratitude. We are committed to the improvement of self, the responsibility of family, and the betterment of our community and the world. Through our venture philanthropy model of giving, we partner with early-stage organizations that demonstrate high leverage, scalable, and sustainable principles. For more information about the David Weekley Family Foundation, visit our website at www.dwf.foundation.

RELATED WORKS

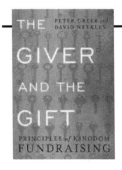

For many people, "fundraising is a dirty word. It conjures up images of guilt-inducing gimmickry and saps the joy from both the donor and the receiver. But what if fundraising has the potential to be good for the giver, not just the recipient? In *The Giver and the Gift,* Peter Greer and David Weekley outline a kingdom, relationship-focused perspective on fundraising. Order your copy at giverandgift.com.

Why do so many organizations—including churches—drift from their founding mission? In *Mission Drift,* HOPE International executives Peter Greer and Chris Horst share how to determine whether your organization is in danger of drift while providing tools to keep organizations "mission true" or get them back on track. Order your copy at missiondrift.com.

66390453R00082

Made in the USA
Lexington, KY
13 August 2017